How to Hook Your Kids on Fishing

Fishing with Small Fry

28/47

DISCARDED

Bob Ellsberg

Flying Pencil Publications
Portland, Oregon

Illustrations © 1991 by Flying Pencil Publications

Published by Flying Pencil Publications
P.O. Box 19062
Portland, Oregon 97219

Electronic Pre-press by Advanced Reprographics, Beaverton, OR
Printed by Artline Printing, Beaverton, OR

Manufactured in the United States of America

10 9 8 7 6 5 4 3 2 1

Cover and Book Design by Mary Stupp-Greer
Technical Illustrations by Kari Valley
Photographs by:
Phil Bullard p. 83; Dan Casali p. 107; Deke Meyer p.1;
Bill Wagner pp. 5, 19, 23, 49, 69, 77, 115; ODFW pp. 39, 89, 99, 103.

Library of Congress Cataloging-in-Publication Data

Ellsberg, Bob, 1947-
   Fishing with small fry : how to hook your kids on fishing
      / Bob Ellsberg.
      p.   cm.
   ISBN 0-916473-07-4 : $9.95
   1. Fishing. 2. Fishing—Study and teaching. I. Title.
SH441.E42 1991
   799.1—dc20   CIP 90-26304

*To the Moms and Dads, Grandpas and Grandmas,
Aunts and Uncles, and other caring friends who strive to
pass on their love of angling to the children of the world.*
*And to the two youngsters who provide much of the
"field testing" for my work (my boys, Steven and Andrew)
and the fine lady who trusted me with them when they were
much too young to be left in my care.*

Contributing Artists

Boise Elliot Elementary
School, Portland, OR
Teacher: Pat Smith

Front row (l. to r.): Alex Yoder,
Tasnim Schatz, Sheila Childers;
Middle row (l. to r.): Alan San-
ders, Jennifer Whitcomb, Josh
Moskovitz, Abigail Maxfield;
Back row (l. to r.): Marie Rogers,
Brandon Schjoth, Wendy Jack-
son, Tanasha Mason

Raleigh Hills Elementary
School, Beaverton,OR
Teachers: Alice Guthrie,
Cathy Gwinn

Front row (l. to r.): Jessie
Moreno, Melanie Mills, Tony
Chavon, Elena Puha;
Middle row (l. to r.): Josh
Spencer, Meghan McDonald;
Back row (l. to r.): Molly
Emmons, Allison Wong
Not shown: Kevin Matulef, Taryn
Howe

Chapman Elementary
School, Sheridan,OR
Teacher: Janet Mautner

Front row (l. to r.): Greg Lux,
Scott Mahe, Christopher Noel,
Rachael Sheperd;
Middle row (l. to r.): Brett
Brower, J.J. Schiesl, Jacob Bran-
son, Bryan Ballantyne, Jill Smiley
Back row (l. to r.): Emily Fabbry,
Jamie Brickell, Jenni Ashcroft,
Cindi Moore, Stacy Freitas
Not shown: Arnold Reed

Jill Smiley
age 10

 Contents

Sheila Childers
age 9

Fish

scaly, shiny
jumping, swimming, hiding
jumping free in the air
splashing

Introduction

Deke Meyer

This book is written for anyone who wants to introduce a youngster to fishing. If you already fish, you'll be ahead of the game. But I am going to assume that many of you are newcomers to the sport—or that you came to fishing as adults (perhaps at a fairly technical level) and have little acquaintance with the likes of crappie, crawdads, nightcrawlers, and other mainstays of childhood angling.

I hope that the skilled fly angler, the grizzled fishing grandparent, and the inexperienced (but game!) single mom will all find information and inspiration here. You can do it, even if this is your own introduction to fishing as well, and you all can have a great time in the process.

We will explore how to fish, but we will concentrate on how to successfully take kids fishing. Providing a successful introduction to fishing is a wonderful gift to give a child, and like all truly wonderful gifts, it does not come cheap. It will cost you quite a bit of time (in thoughtful planning, in preparation, in execution, and away from your own pursuit of fish or other hobbies!). It will cost you a lot of patience. But fortunately it will not require a great deal of money.

Fishing with Small Fry

If you are still wondering whether or not fishing is right for you and your kids, I offer my own (certainly biased) view that fishing is endlessly fascinating, educational, and challenging. It encourages the development of dexterity, requires thought and problem-solving, and provides the excitement of actually catching something, a reward which has thrilled young and old for thousands of years. It offers a flexible, year-around excuse to get out in the fresh air, and can be the focus of a lifetime of adventures.

Nothing is more natural to a youngster than enjoying the outdoors. A million years of evolution have distilled a human race with a pronounced fondness for getting out of the cave and into the environment. When the weather cooperates, most of us—big and small—just naturally prefer the outdoors to the confines of a house.

Like many new parents, I quickly learned that the best way to quiet a screaming little monster was a quick sojourn into the front yard. That same miserable critter who refused to be placated indoors suddenly assumed a whole different countenance. Craning his little neck to get a clear view of the surrounding fauna and flora, my little fella was now actually worth keeping. Sure, his mom was screaming at me to get him out of the rain, but hey, the kid was happy. We'd stay out till his blankie was dripping!

Fishing appeals to a youngster's natural hunter-gatherer instincts. Enthusiasm for berry picking, rock hounding, and all kinds of stalking (from mushrooms to butterflies) can easily be incorporated into fishing expeditions for a change of pace. Furthermore, there's nothing vague about fishing. It focuses on a definite goal—catching a fish—and offers many opportunities for success.

One of fishing's most endearing qualities is that you can talk and angle at the same time. Try explaining the seasons to a youngster while water skiing, or giving a spiel on peer pressure while rock climbing! Fishing provides a good mix of activity and action, with time for reflection and discussion.

If you are an angler yourself, I'll bet you can still remember who first took you fishing and some of your earliest catches. The successful catching of a fish is a significant triumph for a youngster, and the approval gained adds at least an inch of height to any tow-head.

I wrote this book to share with you my own experience as both student (of my granddad) and teacher (of my two sons). I hope you will find it helpful as you encourage your small fry's enjoyment of the outdoors and cultivate their attitude toward sport fishing. If you let them learn at their own pace, and in their own way, they will one day treasure the time they spent with you and love you for it. After a time, they may even let you catch a fish or two!

Jenni Ashcroft
age 10

- 3 -

Fishing with Small Fry

Kevin Matulef
age 11

1
Taking Kids Fishing

A Question of Attitude

Bill Wagner

If you want to have a successful outing with your young charges, you have to have the proper mind set. Go out to the waters with the wrong attitude, and you are doomed to an afternoon of pure misery!

First, you have to keep in mind the difference between "going fishing with the kids" and "taking the kids fishing." While the semantics may seem trivial, the significance is earth shaking. You can "go fishing with the kids" when they are old enough to give you a lift to the lake! Then you can kick back, have a good time, actually try to catch a fish or two yourself, and bore them with stories of their early adventures. Until they attain the age and skills needed for independence, it's best that you clearly identify your efforts as "taking the kids fishing." It's a full time job, so reconcile yourself to putting your own fishing pleasure on the back burner during the process.

The goal of any outdoor activity with children should be to have a good time and enjoy the woods, meadows, and waters. Don't let catching (or trying to catch!) fish get in the way of having a good time. Get obsessive about the actual act of fishing and you run the danger of losing the interest of your companions. Have everything ready for them to use and enjoy, but let them take their pleasures where they will.

During one of my early fishing trips with my eldest son Steven, we got sidetracked during a spring steelhead outing when Steve got caught up in the excitement of a stagnant pond near the parking lot. We spent nearly an hour watching salamanders and polliwogs. By the time we got to the stream, he was all fired up for a little adventure and spent most of the next hour climbing trees and skipping rocks. Eventually, he grew a little tired of these pursuits, and we actually did a little casting and retrieving for a couple of minutes before he suggested that we head off to McDonalds for lunch!

Did we have a great fishing trip? You bet! Steve spent the next few days bragging to all his little buddies about the great fishing trip he had with Dad. I have to admit, the trip won't go down in my *Great Moments in Steelheading* book, but it was a pretty great moment to be a dad.

Most kids have an incredibly short attention span. While you might get lucky and have a youngster who will be content to watch the flow of the water and the motion of the bobber, most prefer a lot of activity. When the action isn't cooperatively provided by the fish, it's best to have plan "B" ready to implement. A little prior planning will keep the outing exciting even during the slowest bite.

Be sure to bring along a substantial picnic basket full of interesting snacks. A quantity and variety of goodies can save the day. I even sneak in a few munchies that are frowned upon for regular consumption at the kitchen table.

Furthermore, strange as it may seem, any longtime angler will tell you that the fish bite best when your concentration wanders. Stuffing one's face is a time proven way to spur fish into action!

Bring along a few favorite toys. When the kids were real little, I'd always tuck away a favorite blanket and chew toy or rattle. As they grew more mobile, we graduated to balls, frizbees, and kites. If you pick a fishing hole with good beach access or a nearby field, you can encourage the kids to burn off some energy during those times when the fish are "resting." As the kids burn out, it doesn't hurt to have a few stories to read. A sunny day on a shady dock is the perfect setting for a few tales of adventure.

Above all, be honest with yourself. Keep your goals simple, your expectations realistic, and don't underestimate the size of the commitment you're undertaking. Youngsters on an outing are a real handful. You'll have to handle all of the equipment, make sure that everything from diapers to doughnuts is accounted for, and still be available to give the kids a great deal of attention, for safety as well as success.

Allison Wong
age 9

Fishing with Small Fry

Jill Smiley
age 10

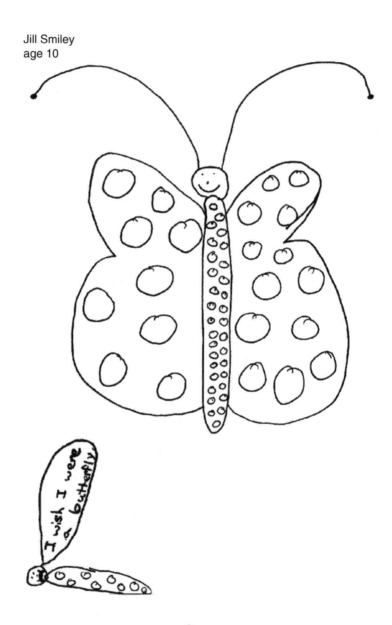

I wish I were a butterfly

2
Bring 'em Back Alive (and Happy)

Safety Considerations

Oregon Dept. of Fish and Wildlife

The outdoors is a wonderful place, but there are a number of dangers that should be acknowledged and considered before you head for the fishin' hole.

Water is our most exciting element. It thrills us, intrigues us, and relaxes us. Unfortunately, it can also drown us if we aren't careful. My wife would lose a lot of her enthusiasm for my outings with our boys if I came back with fewer young'uns than I took!

For safety's sake, you'll want to give some thought to the setting for your fishing adventures with children. The terrain associated with water can vary tremendously. Be sure to select a setting suitable to the age and competence of your little fishing buddies.

Some areas are only suitable for adults, some for only fit adults. Most ocean jetties and rocky shorelines should be off limits for kids under eight. Many of these breakwaters are made of riprap (large chunks of broken boulders and cement) and are treacherous under the best of circumstances. If you're really careful, you might be able to haul a munchkin out to the jetty. But the fishing will be too difficult for real participation, and there is absolutely no place to run and play if boredom sets in.

For little ones, it's best to look for calm water with gradually sloping beaches or banks. Steep drop-offs or strong currents make constant body to body contact a necessity, which will spoil the fun for both adult and child. I prefer a place with open beaches where the kids will have to run several steps to get into significant water. That gives me lots of yelling (and if necessary, running) time.

Take enough adults to insure that the kids will be under adequate surveillance. I'd never venture out alone with more than one child under four, unless one was tiny and safely tucked into my backpack. Little kids who fall into

Melanie Mills
age 11

the "mindless but fully mobile" category need to have a quick adult supervisor on alert at all times. Once children hit five or so, they may or may not be manageable. I've actually taken out several five-year-olds with success, but it's best to have a high adult to child ratio if you foresee control problems.

If there is deep water present, put the younger kids in good life jackets. There are styles available now that are pretty comfortable and won't make a kid hot and miserable, an important consideration in itself. Never install a child in an untested lifejacket. Test the effectiveness of a jacket by putting it on its wearer, and plunking the two of them into a pool or calm body of water. They should float, preferably head up!

A couple of years ago, one of my hunter safety classes rescued a three year old who had been allowed to wade the shoreline of one of our local lakes wearing an oversized jacket. Not surprisingly, the little girl eventually slipped into the water and was soon floating beautifully with her head six inches below the waterline. Cheaply made or poorly fitting flotation devices can be death traps.

While water is always a major concern on any fishing adventure, there are other lesser dangers that, while rarely life threatening, can certainly ruin the fun for both youngsters and their adults.

The sun generally makes a happy contribution to an outing on a summer day, but it can quickly burn fair skinned little ones to an uncomfortable crisp when its ultraviolet rays are magnified by reflection from the water. Really young children, especially first year babies, must be fully protected at all times. Don't be fooled by the hour of the day. Mornings and late afternoons (and even thin cloud covers) can easily produce enough sun to turn pale ones a spooky shade of crimson.

I still vividly remember one of my own early pack trips to a high country lake in the Sierras. Our all male troupe had managed to make it up to a hidden lake at some 10,000 feet elevation. We all stripped down to our under-shorts and spent the whole afternoon lazing on the rocks in the lake, angling for beautiful Eastern brook trout. That night I felt like I had been fried in deep fat. None of us could move easily or wear tight clothing for three days. The memories of that trip have little to do with fishing!

Fortunately there are good sunscreens on the market, including several that are waterproof. Try to get the lotion on before you leave, and be sure to cover every square inch that might be exposed.

Rachael Shepherd
age 10

My grandpa always let me choose a favorite good luck cap before each season. Naturally, I'd wear that sucker until mom wouldn't let it in the house. We'd buy cute fishing pins for the brim and decorate it. But Grandpa knew it was more than just a lucky charm. It helped to keep my noggin safe and comfortable all summer, preventing sunburn and headaches from too much glare in the eyes.

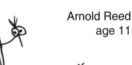

Arnold Reed
age 11

Another potential trip-spoiler is insects. Where there is water, there is buggies. A lot of these flying and crawling critters are fun to watch and provide great entertainment. Some make good bait, and others encourage the fish to acrobatics that provide major excitement among anglers of all ages. Unfortunately, a few also look upon fishermen, young and old, as little more than a convenient lunch.

The most common of these biters are mosquitoes. The females of the species need a good snort of red blood to provide nourishment for their spawning efforts, and anglers seem to offer a preferred vintage. Mosquitoes must have still water to reproduce. In the mountains during spring and early summer, hordes of these obnoxious rascals breed in potholes of snowmelt. They also thrive in swampy low-lands during any season free of frost. While mosquitoes swarm primarily in the evening, they can attack at any time. If it's calm and warm, you may be in trouble! A good wind will keep them off, and getting out onto the lake in a boat may offer refuge from mosquito infested shores.

Other airborne attackers include biting gnats (commonly called no-see-ums) and a whole variety of nasty flies. If your locale is cursed with a healthy population of these little buggers, you should always pack a good insect repellent along with your gear.

Some repellents actually work. Unfortunately, the stronger brands can cause rashes and other allergic reactions on smaller children and should be home tested in small quantities before using wholesale during a stream-side attack. Airborne attackers of all varieties can be deterred to an extent by dressing to minimize chewable areas. Blue jeans and tightly woven long sleeve canvas shirts will keep a lot of skin off the menu, and reduce sun and wind exposure as well.

Brandon Schjoth, age 9

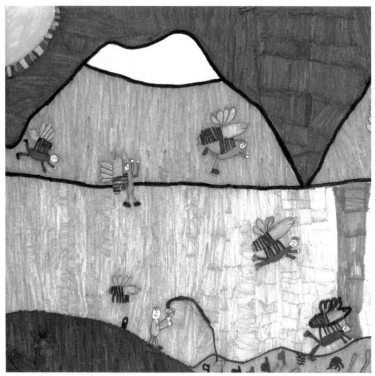

If the bugs are really awful, and repellant is ineffective or the kids are allergic, hats with net masks are available. It is unlikely, however, that a youngster is going to be amused for long by dressing up as a beekeeper, so you're probably better off packing it in for the day, planning to return after the hatch has passed.

Less common, but far worse than mosquitoes and gnats, are the variety of wasps, hornets, and bees that nest most everywhere. These insects can be big trouble, inflicting painful bites and stings, and often attacking in large numbers if disturbed. The best plan is obviously to avoid disturbing them. Unlike the biters that are actually looking for a meal, bees and wasps usually attack only when provoked (such as stepping on them or disturbing their nest). However, wasps and hornets can get just plain ornery in the fall, and should be especially avoided at that time.

Since most bees and wasps nest in trees or in holes in the ground, sticking close to the bank usually insures you fairly safe passage. Unfortunately, some areas next to the water seem to be favorite drinking spots for bees and should be avoided.

While most stings and bites are painful, they are rarely life threatening. Conveniently packaged bottles of balm for stings are available, and will take away some of the itch and pain. Their effectiveness is limited, but they do give you something you can provide, and that is often all it takes to comfort a little one.

For a few of us, however, bee and wasp stings are very dangerous and can lead to death. Those who have allergic reactions to stings may suffer shortness of breath and dizziness after an attack and must be rushed promptly to a hospital. If previous problems have been diagnosed, be sure to get a special kit from your doctor, and add it to your standard first aid kit.

A far sneakier beastie that can cause harm is the tick. These little beetle-like critters hang in the foliage and drop on any warm blooded critter that walks past and releases a little carbon dioxide. They like to sneak under clothes and dig into your hide. I generally find my little passengers after my trips when I'm taking a shower. They do hold on tight but can be encouraged to back out of your skin by application of a little lighter fluid or other volatile substance such as rubbing alcohol. One favorite technique is to put a hot match to their exposed parts, but since "theirs" are in close proximity to "mine" that is not my favorite approach!

Tick inflicted wounds should be cleaned with antiseptic and watched carefully. Unfortunately, ticks can carry sicknesses such as lyme disease and Rocky Mountain spotted fever, so you might want to check with your doctor if you or the kids feel unwell after playing host to a tick or two.

In some areas (few in the U.S.), spiders and snakes can cause occasional anxious moments. Fortunately, these critters are shy by nature and will avoid humans if at all possible. With the exception of the black widow spider, almost all spider bites are less harmful than that of a bee, and the black widow is almost always hidden away under rocks or buildings.

If your fishing grounds serve as habitat for venomous snakes, give your young partners a little lecture on the wisdom of avoiding likely hiding places before the trip. If you are more than an hour or so from a hospital, you might consider packing a snake bite kit along. While very few bites of even the most dangerous American snakes are

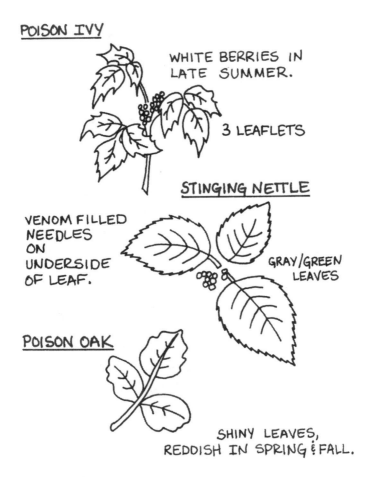

POISON IVY

WHITE BERRIES IN LATE SUMMER.

3 LEAFLETS

STINGING NETTLE

VENOM FILLED
NEEDLES
ON
UNDERSIDE
OF LEAF.

GRAY/GREEN
LEAVES

POISON OAK

SHINY LEAVES,
REDDISH IN SPRING & FALL.

fatal, they can make a child pretty sick, and prompt medical attention is always in order.

As if all of these fighting fauna weren't enough, you might also run into a few species of "attack plants" as well. While all unknown berries should be avoided, most problems come from contact with plants that irritate the skin. The most common of these, poison oak and ivy, can cause nasty rashes that appear a day or so after the adventure and can cause discomfort for a couple of weeks. Since they don't sting or itch on contact to warn their victims away, it's important that you learn to recognize them before your outing. When you spot them during an outing, draw the children's attention to them, pointing out their distinguishing characteristics.

I always wear a good deal of protective clothing if I'm hiking through the stuff, and wash thoroughly with a good soap afterwards. There are also medicines available to immunize you and the youngsters if you are planning an outing to an infested area. But the best precaution is to avoid these menacing greens. Most people have a very low (or no) tolerance for them, and the rashes that result can cause such misery that it's not worth the risk.

I happen to have a better than average tolerance for poison oak and ivy, but I do get nailed by another real nasty—stinging nettles. These tall green guys grow next to a lot of my favorite streams and blend insidiously with other common vegetation. Within minutes (sometimes seconds!) of contact, they raise blisters on my skin that sting and itch for several unforgettable hours! As with the other poison plants, some people react less violently to this one, experiencing only a startling stinging or burning sensation. Fortunately, even for me, nettles don't cause long lasting discomfort, but they can still ruin an outing for the little ones. Know what these nuisances look like, and keep clear.

Allison Wong
age 9

3
Getting Started

Resources You Can Tap

Bill Wagner

Children, especially those under ten, rarely care about what is actually caught. There is something mysterious and wonderful about actually dredging something (anything) up from the depths. The same "trash fish" or "bait stealer" that is scorned by their elders can bring great satisfaction to novice anglers.

Keep in mind that children have little patience and a great need for success. Give them action and success early. They will develop sophistication in time.

The best fish to try for will be small and plentiful. Small size is a must for little fishermen. Large fish are scary to a little tyke, and playing and landing the larger species can require a bravery that few youngsters can muster. Pan fish (such as sunfish and blue gills) are my favorite choice for the very young. These little fish travel in large schools, are ready biters, feed near the surface, and do a lot of splashing around. They don't have sharp fins that can hurt little fingers, and are tough enough to withstand a little rough play from the youngsters.

Bryan Ballantyne
age 11

Trout are also good quarry, especially in lakes and ponds that are regularly stocked by the state fishery folks. "Grandpa" fish hiding in swift streams and rivers may be pretty sophisticated, but newly released hatchery reared rainbow and cutthroat trout will bite at almost anything. These hatchery plants offer a manageable fight and are a good first eating fish as well. Easiest fishing is immediately after the hatchery truck leaves the premises! To find out what the stocking schedule is for your area, or for a specific water, contact your local office of the state fish and wildlife agency.

Living in the Northwest, my kids have lots of chances to catch salmon, steelhead, sturgeon, and trout. So what are their favorites? In the coastal rivers they love the little three to five inch sculpin that are common throughout tidewater. Sculpin are ugly as toads, of no food value, and provide a very short fight. But they are willing biters and will stay alive for hours in a bucket and still swim happily away after we're through. In salt water my boys' favorite is flounder. These flat fish respond with hard tugs, fight in short little spurts, and look a lot like little sea monsters to the kids! What could be better?

Where to Go

If you have absolutely no pride and just want to give your kids a good quick taste of fishing, you might consider taking them to a fish farm. Here, for a set price per fish (or inch), you can buy the kids the experience of feeling a fish on the line. These ponds are thickly populated, and the action is fast. The kids will haul in enough catch to bankrupt you in no time! Now I'm not saying that this is very sporting, but it may be just the teaser you need to get your kids excited about future adventures in a more natural setting.

As you begin your search for the perfect place, remember: you are looking for a safe, easily accessible spot where fish are plentiful and easy to catch. If you are new to the game yourself (or to the area) there are a number of local information sources you can tap. The sporting goods store is one. If your community is blessed with an old fashioned, smelly little bait shop, that is definitely your best bet. Folks who run places called "Joe's Bait" generally know what's what. The clerks at the sporting goods department of the variety store are also worth a shot.

Fishing clubs are another good source of where-to-go information. Members are generally delighted to welcome newcomers to their favorite sport, offer advice freely, and may even invite you and your youngsters on an outing. To find fishing clubs in your area, check with the Chamber of Commerce, the sporting goods store, or the local office of your state fish and wildlife agency.

Attend an Outdoor Show. In addition to displaying all kinds of fishing equipment, outdoor shows offer the chance to tap many local information sources (sporting goods stores, equipment manufacturers, fishing clubs, as well as state agencies have information booths at these shows). Take your little buddies along. Many of the shows set up artificial fish ponds especially for kids. The "ponds" (actually, tanks) are stocked with hungry fish, and the kids can usually haul out a couple at no charge.

Other sources of where-to-go recommendations are the local office of the state fish and wildlife agency, the municipal (or state) parks department, or even the sports writer (or outdoor columnist) at the local newspaper.

Some communities actually have "kids only" ponds. Not only is competition there light and the waters generally well stocked, but the kids will meet anglers their own height whose experience and expertise might inspire them. Within an outing or two, yours may well be sharing fish stories and swapping lies!

Tasnim Schatz
age 8

4
Tackle for Tots

Rods, Reels, and Lines

Bill Wagner

Few states require licenses for those under twelve, but start-up expenses for your new angler will vary, depending on the equipment you choose to buy. You can catch fish on as little as a piece of string and a chunk of bait. In most cases, however, fishing involves some sort of rod or pole (fishermen who buy expensive rods never say "pole"), a reel, a line, and a hook. For many kinds of fishing, weights are also necessary.

A vivid memory of my own youth is an afternoon on a muddy river catching sunfish perch on a piece of string with a little bacon tied to the end. We had set out to catch a few crawfish. We'd lower the bacon to the bottom (weighted with a tiny split shot sinker), wait till we felt a little movement, and then would slowly lift the clinging crawfish up to the dock. Eventually this activity attracted a large school of sunfish, and we decided to try to catch a few.

Since the perch were schooling near the surface, we removed our sinkers and tried to find something to use as a hook. While some of our group began scrounging for a paper clip or safety pin, a couple of us tried fishing with just the tied up bacon. Sure enough, the greedy perch bit the bacon and held on fast, refusing to let go of the bait as we pulled them within grabbing distance!

Handlines

A HANDLINE IS PERFECT FOR CATCHING SMALL FISH OFF A PIER.

One of my preferred fishing outfits when I was a kid was a little green handline. Wrapped around a framework of wood, the handline was best used from piers that reached out to deep water, or from boats. As we were already in deep water to start with, no casting was required. Holding the line in one's fingers gives a new fisherman an excellent feel for the action below. Every little nibble is translated directly to the fingers holding the line.

A handline can easily be tucked into one's pocket, and it travels well in the glove box of the car. But it has its drawbacks. If casting is required to reach deep water, one can attach a little lead to the line and circle it overhead, releasing it like a cowboy roping

a steer. Unless your budding rodeo champs are pretty coor-
dinated, they may toss it back on shore or end up hooking
an ear—possibly yours!

You should also consider that if anything much heavier
than a pound or two hits the handline, fingers may be in
trouble. A rod or pole will absorb the impact of a large fish
and help play the critter. With a handline, the technique is
to very quickly pay out line. True enough, Hemmingway's
hero in *The Old Man and the Sea* used a handline to catch
his huge marlin, but his hands were calloused by a lifetime
at sea, and he still cut himself up something awful.

Monsters of the deep aside, a handline is a great way to
catch little fish off a pier, and a fun way to start. When I
was about eight years old, I took my little green handline
down to one of my favorite fishing piers on the central
California coast. I had managed to find a few sand crabs
on the beach and had stored them away in my pants pockets.

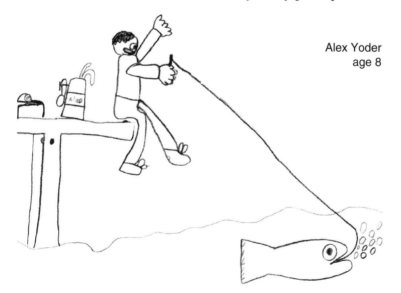

Alex Yoder
age 8

Fishing with Small Fry

A good number of adult fishermen, equipped with heavy rods and reels, were fishing on the pier when I arrived. They were having little luck. They chuckled at me as I pulled the handline from my jacket pocket and lowered it slowly into the blue water near the piling.

Naturally, the other fishermen were using their outfits to cast far away from the pier. Fortunately for me, the fish were mostly feeding next to the pilings. Within an hour, I had landed a dozen big rainbow perch, which I generously gave to my less successful angling colleagues on the dock when it was time for me to get back to our campground. You don't forget days like that.

Pole and Bobber

Many a youngster has learned to fish using a simple long stick with a string tied to the end. The best pole material (for this is definitely a "pole") is long, relatively light, and pliable. Bamboo (also called "cane") has long been considered ideal for the effort. A line is tied to the thinner end, and sinker, hook, and bobber are attached. With an eight foot long pole you can get your line out pretty far into a pond or river. No reel is involved, and the cast is nothing more that swinging the weighted line out into the water.

If a fish pulls the rod tip down or hauls the bobber under, the angler need only lift the pole to vertical position, and the fish come flying at you! Nothing much to tangle, no problems with drag or reel handles, and anyone can soon master the technique.

These outfits will serve your youngsters quite well in areas where the fish are within ten feet, and are near the surface. Panfish such as crappie, bluegill, and perch are excellent species for cane pole angling. Much bigger species can be taken, however. The rods used for commercially catching giant tuna are nothing more than a stouter rod with a heavier line and hook attached. For some of the really huge fish, several rods and lines are connected to a single hook. Since the hungry tuna are boiling right next to the boat, a reel would just complicate the whole affair. Your little fishermen won't be handling anything the size of a tuna, but the simplicity of a cane pole and line is an excellent way to start.

Rod and Reel

Most anglers use some combination of rod and reel. For the best action, most fish, and most fun, the outfit used should be geared to the fish pursued and to the size and skill of the user. My grandfather, who taught me the ropes, was a firm believer in "bigger is better." A true depression fisherman, he always made sure we had plenty of extra power in our rods and reels. When we were fishing for catfish, we always had gear that could handle any five

Brandon Schjoth
age 9

Catfish

- 27 -

hundred pound sturgeon that happened our way! We never had a fish break off, but we might have had a little more fun with a lighter outfit.

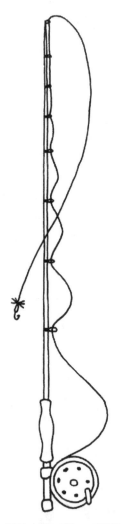

FLY CASTING OUTFIT

On the other hand, a young angler using gear that is too light may get tired, discouraged, and even a little scared if the line is screaming off the reel and the fish refuses to come in. Ask your sporting goods clerk to help you match gear to angler, keeping in mind the fish you intend to pursue.

A rod serves three major functions. First, it helps cast out the bait or lure. The shorter the casting distance needed, the shorter the rod can be. Second, a rod helps you feel the activity in the water. The rod tip will bend if pulled, and the rod will transmit the movement of the line to your fingers. Certain rods are built to maximize the feel, while others assume that the fish will give a good enough pull to make its presence known.

Finally, a rod helps you play the fish. Much of a fish's action can be absorbed by the bending and flexing of the rod. Like a long skinny shock absorber, the rod relieves the line (and one's hands) of much of the strain of the struggling fish. Anglers using light lines with big fish appreciate the help that a long flexible rod can give them. If, however, you are fishing from a boat or pier and need to be able to move the fish around (especially in a crowd of other anglers), a shorter, heavier rod may be just the ticket. Not only does that rod give you good control, but you aren't as likely to poke one of the other fishermen in the eye!

Small children should use rather short rods whenever possible. The smaller size gives them more control and allows you to mess with their bait and tackle more easily. Shorter rods are less likely to get wedged in between boards or poked in sister's eye. A child can also see the rod tip more easily with a short rod and watch for nibbles at closer range.

There are a great number of rods on the market today. They range in length from a couple of feet to ten feet and more. They are made of a wide variety of materials, including aluminum, fiberglass, graphite, and boron. The different materials affect their weight, flexibility, and cost. Fish that bite very lightly, or fishing techniques that require a delicate touch, may require the light sensitivity of graphite. Other species that greedily grab the bait and run can very well be caught on less expensive materials. A good quality fiberglass rod is inexpensive, suitable for most situations, and more resistant to breakage than rods built from exotic (and costly) materials.

Rods are designed to work with a specific type and weight of reel, and differ in the location of the reel seat and the size, type, and spacing of the rod guides. If you are unsure of your needs, a knowledgeable salesperson will work to assure that your rod and reel are compatible. If you've already got the reel, bring it along when you go to purchase the rod. Dealers that specialize in fishing gear usually hire folks that understand tackle. If you're shopping at discount stores, bring along an angling friend.

Reels

All reels serve the function of storing the line, but there are many kinds of reels to choose from. They differ in their capacity to hold the line and in the way that they feed the line out when casting. Baitcasting and spinning reels use the weight of the sinker or lure to pull line from the spool, while flycasting reels are more primitive, generally consisting simply of a moveable spool with a hand crank on its side.

A fly angler uses a casting motion and the weight of the line to carry the fly out over the water. Instead of feeding out all at once, fly line is pulled from the reel by the angler and kept in the air by the casting motion.

Contrary to popular opinion, one doesn't need to be an expert angler to cast or fish with fly fishing gear. But fly fishing is usually difficult for young beginners, with a longer lead time between first effort and first fish in the net. Fly fishing skills are best learned after one is hooked on fishing and has experienced a little success using simpler methods. A youngster first needs enough interest, then enough patience, to work on the skills necessary to enjoy fly fishing. Almost all communities in America have fly fishing clubs that are happy to welcome youngsters to the sport, and will provide the instruction and equipment to get them started.

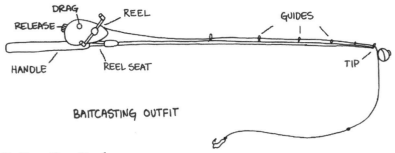

DRAG
RELEASE
REEL
GUIDES
HANDLE
REEL SEAT
TIP
BAITCASTING OUTFIT

Baitcasting Reels

A very simple reel to understand and operate is the casting (or baitcasting) reel. This reel features an open spool that rolls forward to feed out line. Most of these reels have a spool release that allows the reel to spin freely when cast. The release can then be locked when the desired length of line has played out. They also have a feature called a drag that lets even a locked spool play out line when a certain amount of pressure is applied. Usually, the drag weight is set just a little less than the breaking strength of the line used. If the fish is pulling really hard, the drag feeds out line before the line is in danger of breaking.

Casting reels are commonly used for fishing from charter boats and for other activities that demand a tough, reliable reel that is easy to operate. Casting the reel usually requires some practice. One must learn to let the reel spin while maintaining enough pressure with the thumb to prevent backlash. This unhappy event occurs when the line spool spins so quickly that it exceeds the line's ability to clear the spool. When the lure or bait slows as it hits the water, the spool is still spinning like crazy. If you don't slow it down with your thumb, the line will create a huge ball of looped, snarled line around the reel spool. This "bird nest" may take hours to untangle. A little casting practice will alleviate this problem, but even the best angler sometimes snarls the reel. Some reels have a magnetic device that reduces, but does not eliminate, this tendency.

Kids ten or over can master a baitcasting reel with a bit of practice. These reels are tough, and will handle a good quantity of heavy line if you are fishing for larger species.

Spinning Reels

Spinning reels are much easier to cast without tangles. These reels come in a variety of closed face (where you can't see the line; it comes out a little hole) and open faced models. Spinning reel spools don't move during the cast. The line, which is going out perpendicular to the spool, feeds off freely with no help from the fisherman, and because the spool is stationary, backlash is eliminated. A spinning reel is usually a good choice for a first outfit.

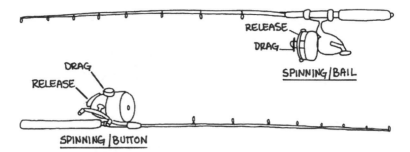

RODS AND REELS COME IN DIFFERENT STYLES AND WEIGHTS. MATCH YOUR REEL TO THE RIGHT ROD.

The two most popular spinning reel styles I call the button and the bail. The button reel, popularized by Zebco™, has a closed face and can be cast by pushing and then releasing a large button in the back of the reel. This is the type of reel I used as a little kid for trout and small fish. The line is hidden behind a metal covering and comes out a tiny hole in the front. The action is simple, it's almost impossible to snarl, and the better quality reels will last a long time. When it does snarl, however, the closed housing makes freeing the line a bit more complicated.

The most popular type of spinning reel is the open-faced bail model. The line is threaded under a bail and out the rod guides. Pressure against the bail keeps the line from feeding out. To cast, one must lift or "open" the bail, hold the strand of line against the rod, and then cast the bait and release the line at the same time. This sounds a little complicated—and is. Most kids under seven or eight have trouble mastering the motion. But with a little practice, even younger children can learn the skill.

Open-faced bail operated reels are a little more fragile than those without bails and do require a bit more maintenance. They are, however, available in a variety of prices and sizes and are a good choice for many kinds of fishing.

One of the most difficult decisions a parent will make is whether to buy one of the inexpensive "kid reels," or to spring for a little higher quality. It has been my experience that you are better off spending a few extra bucks and buying quality. The really cheap reels usually don't last or work at all well. Kids don't enjoy their fishing nearly as much if the reel doesn't cast properly.

It is usually a bad idea to buy your kids outfits that are a lot different than the one you are planning to use. If you have upgraded equipment, even the youngest child will soon catch on and want to use yours, even if it's too hard to handle.

During my college years, I worked as a counselor in a camp for underprivileged kids near Hunter's Point in San Francisco. One summer, the camp director decided that we should take the kids fishing at Lake Merced, a popular fishing spot right in the city. We worked for a few days making simple rods and lines for the kids. When the fish-

Jacob Branson
age 11

ing day arrived, I decided that I'd take along my new spinning outfit and give it a try. The lake was very heavily fished, and I had no interest in doing much catching, but I thought I'd try out my gear before I took a planned pack trip later that summer.

Soon after we arrived, we set up the kids' outfits and started them fishing. They really couldn't cast their lines very far, but they were having a good time. After my kids were in the water, I put together my outfit, tied on a heavy (if inappropriate) spinner, and took a cast far out into the lake. After only a couple of cranks, something substantial smacked my swirling brass lure. A few minutes later, a fat twenty-two inch trout was flopping on the bank.

Needless to say, that was the last I saw of my outfit that day. All the kids immediately lost interest in their tackle and wanted to try mine. Unfortunately, the fish had been a fluke (as well as a trout!), and nothing else was landed on hook and line that afternoon. (The kids did quite well catching fish bare handed as they were released from a planter truck later that day!)

If you can, borrow a few different outfits from friends for your kids to try. If you are an expert angler yourself, you may well have forgotten how hard it is to get a line out into the water the first time. Let the kids try casting in the yard. If they like a certain kind of outfit and can use it reasonably well, it will probably make a good purchase. Even for new fisherfolk, confidence in one's gear is important.

Most kids will have a lot of fun casting even if there is no action going on in the water. Get something that will work well and last a while. A good outfit will outlast ten junk reels, and probably save you money in the end.

Line

There are two types of line commonly used for fishing: monofilament and braided nylon. Most anglers use monofilament. As the name implies, this line is a single strand of material. It is available in a variety of colors (including white, brown, yellow, and clear) with the intention that it be visible to the angler and (supposedly) invisible to the fish.

Monofilament has very small diameter for its strength. A good deal of line can be put on even the smallest spool. It comes in very light weights, some so thin as to be almost invisible even to the angler's eye. The lightest weights can cast out a bait or lure without spooking even the most alert and timid fish.

Braided nylon is stiffer than monofilament and has less give. It is preferred by anglers in pursuit of very large fish. Braided line does not snarl as easily as monofilament and is less likely to fray and nick. While it is much more visible to fish, it can be used in conjunction with a monofilament leader, thus allowing one to have a very tough line and still keep the area near the bait or lure free from distractions. It takes less of the larger diameter braided line to fill a reel spool, so larger reels are commonly used.

Lines are rated by their breaking strength. For instance, two pound test line should be able to hold two pounds of weight on the line without breaking, fifty pound test should be able to hold fifty, and so on. The actual breaking strength (except when brand new) depends on the condition of the line. Lines lose some of their original strength over time after being subjected to sunlight, abrasion, knots, and stretching. The weakest point in a line is usually found

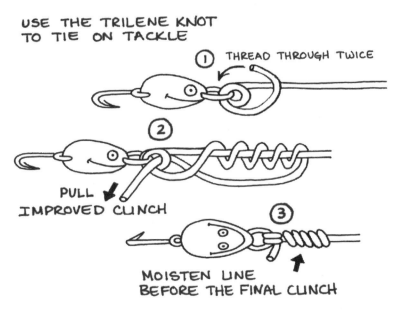

USE THE TRILENE KNOT
TO TIE ON TACKLE

① THREAD THROUGH TWICE

②

PULL

IMPROVED CLINCH

③

MOISTEN LINE
BEFORE THE FINAL CLINCH

at a knot. An overhand (granny) knot in a line will reduce its strength by half. Simple to tie knots designed for mono-filament line are used to preserve the strength of the line.

For practical purposes, the lighter test lines are best used in smaller reels for smaller fish. Heavy lines are more suitable for reels with larger capacity used for larger species. This is a general rule, however, and there are many exceptions. Very large fish can be taken on very light line in the open ocean where no snags create prob-lems and the boat can follow the fish for hours. Rather small fish can merit using heavy lines if they have to be hauled up a jetty or pier, or if they have to be horsed out of heavy brush or weeds as soon as they are hooked.

Another exception to the general rule is the case of new anglers. New anglers chasing relatively small fish are best off with line of about ten pound test. Ten pound test is easy to see and easy to work with when threading rod guides and the eyes of hooks, lures, and bobbers. It is also easier than lighter lines to tie in a variety of simple knots.

Lighter lines tend to tangle and bird nest more easily. Nothing loses a youngster's interest faster than big snarls that take a lot of time to straighten out. An adult's humor rapidly fails after being handed the tenth consecutive fouled reel. Finally, ten pound test is pretty tough stuff. On ten pound line, your young charges can mess up on the reel drag adjustment, get the fish caught in brush, and still manage to haul it up to the dock!

Stacy Freitas
age 11

5
Inside the
Tackle Box

Bobbers, Hooks, Sinkers
and Tools

Oregon Dept. of Fish and Wildlife

Bobbers

While hardly an essential piece of fishing gear, I'm a great believer in using a bobber when fishing with young anglers. A bit of floating material, whether a shiny plastic ball for panfish, or a fifty gallon barrel like that used in *Jaws*, is pretty exciting when it goes under. Small fry fisherfolk may not be able, or willing, to hold the rod still enough to feel a nibble, but they will sure watch the bobber twitch, wobble, and go under with a "Bloop!"

A submerged bobber creates an exquisite moment of panic. One of the great attractions of fishing is this moment of mystery, after the take and before the taker makes itself known. Many a child has been intrigued by Dr. Seuss's classic, *McGilligan's Pool*. The author suggests that all kinds of wondrous monsters may be lurking beneath the waters, and all anglers share the same hopes! A bobber has the effect of magnifying that moment, allowing little ones who are easily distracted to experience the thrill.

Bobbers are now available in a wide variety of shapes and colors, including cartoon characters made of plastic designed especially for youngsters' tackle boxes. (We have yet to see Mickey go under after a bluegill, but he also doubles as a bathtub toy.) The best bobbers to use for fishing are the smallest that can be easily seen. A smaller bobber will dance and go under much more easily, will cause fewer casting problems, and will be less affected by the wind.

BOBBERS
MAKE IT
EASIER
TO SPOT THE
NIBBLE!

PUSH HERE

ATTACH
LINE HERE

Bobbers work best on relatively still bodies of water. Fast flowing rivers or streams will carry the bobber back to the bank before much fishing time elapses. In a calm lake, the bobber will sit for however long it takes to do the job without requiring retrieval and re-casting. In most cases, a worm or other bait can be suspended a couple of feet below the bobber to dangle enticingly for panfish and trout to admire and chomp.

Bobbers are also used to fish deep, even by experienced anglers after larger species. Baits are adjusted so that they are suspended just inches off the bottom by the bobber, which also signals the take.

Another great advantage of a bobber is that it will prevent a young fisherman from reeling the hook all the way into the rod guides when line is being retrieved. Kids will usually reel in their line until the tackle gets jammed in the tip of the rod. A bobber will stop the retrieval and make it relatively easy for you to remove the fish or re-bait. If you are not using a bobber, you should consider attaching a large barrel or snap swivel well above the hook to perform the same function. Be sure that its diameter is larger than that of the guide.

The main disadvantage in using a bobber is that it cuts off the direct link between the rod and the fish. To set a hook into the fish, you first must reel in enough line to give you a direct tie to the bobber, then jerk the rod tip up hard. Hopefully the fish will still be around!

Scott Mahe
age 11

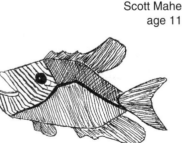

The smaller the bobber, the less problem this will be. But even if you catch fewer fish, a bobber keeps the youngsters excited, and that's enough for me!

Hooks

Mankind has used hooks for thousands of years to catch dinner. Whether made of bone, wood, or metal, the fishhook has been one of the great survival tools of all time. The principle is simple: one fastens a hook on the end of a line and covers it with something that the fish tries to eat. As the fish pulls the hook into its mouth and swims off with its prize, the hook penetrates the flesh of the mouth or stomach, and the fish is held more or less securely until the angler retrieves line, hook, and fish.

In general, hooks have an eye at one end where you tie on your line. Below the eye is a shank (where fly anglers tie on feathers, fur and other stuff). The hook bends in a u-shape and comes to a point. In most cases there is a barb just below the point.

The main purpose of the barb is to restrain the point from slipping out of a hooked fish's mouth, which it may do if the line is allowed to go slack. Once the point of the hook penetrates the fish, the barb resists backing out. A second function of the barb is to retain an impaled piece of bait on the hook, preventing it from sliding off the point.

Fish hooks come in many shapes and sizes, with selection determined by the bait, lure, or fly to be connected to them—and by the size and characteristics of the mouth that will be attacking them.

When fishing with small fry, plan to use small hooks. Most fishermen use much larger hooks than needed, anyway.

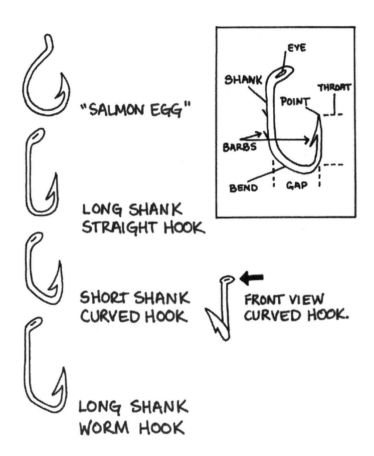

"SALMON EGG"

EYE

SHANK

THROAT

POINT

BARBS

BEND   GAP

LONG SHANK
STRAIGHT HOOK.

SHORT SHANK
CURVED HOOK

FRONT VIEW
CURVED HOOK.

LONG SHANK
WORM HOOK

Very large fish can be caught on relatively small hooks with no problem. The reverse rarely holds true. If you are using large hooks with big chunks of bait, small fish will chew off the bait without getting caught. You'll spend all your time re-baiting with nothing to play, let alone land. Use little hooks, and you'll hook nearly everything that bites—and with kids, any fish is a good fish!

I'd also like to suggest that you consider removing the barbs from your hooks when fishing with kids. This will have a number of desirable effects. First, they will hook more fish. It takes quite a bit more effort to drive a barbed point into a fish than just the point. Many professional anglers recommend barbless fishing for huge fish such as salmon. Their theory is that the increased number of fish hooked without barbs more than makes up for those fish that manage to free themselves.

A second practical benefit is that barbless hooks are easier to free from clothing and—even more important— from young anglers. No matter how careful you are, kids are going to get hooked. A barbed hook is hard to extract from the skin. (In the event of this unhappy occurrence, it is best to cut off the line and head for the nearest emergency room.) If you have removed the barb, however, all you need to do is slide the hook back out.

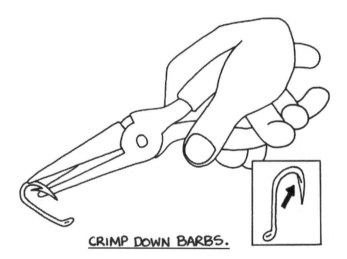

CRIMP DOWN BARBS.

Finally, barbless hooks enable you to release fish you don't want to keep with very little injury to the fish. Barbless hooks are required in more and more fisheries to help preserve low stocks and to encourage catch and release fishing.

Removing the barb from a hook is simple. In most cases, needle nose pliers can be used to flatten the barb against the shank of the hook. With larger hooks one can use a file to remove the barb material.

Many lures now feature several hooks joined together. The most common of these are double or treble hooks. While these look like they should catch more fish, that may not be the case. A single point will penetrate much better than a double or treble hook. With youngsters, the extra hooks are hard to control and often get tangled in the fishing gear, anglers' clothing, and the anglers themselves. Stick with single hooks.

THE LARGER THE NUMBER

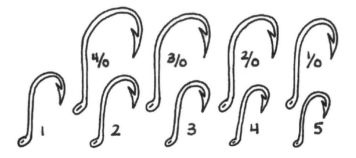

THE SMALLER THE HOOK

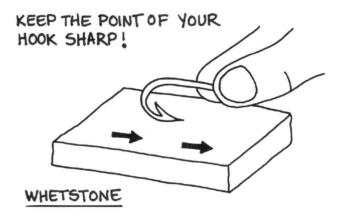

KEEP THE POINT OF YOUR
HOOK SHARP!

WHETSTONE

With all hooks, far better results are obtained if the hook is sharp. Most hooks need a bit of sharpening even when new. A properly sharpened hook will tend to stick when the point is rubbed against your thumbnail. If it doesn't, a few strokes against a hook sharpener or whetstone will usually touch it up. Stroke the hook point against (into) the sharpening surface a few times on each side, and test it again against your thumbnail.

Sinkers

Since primitive times, fisherfolk have realized that a little weight can help the fishing effort. Not only will it drag bait and hook down to where most of the fish live, but it also lets you cast further out into the water.

While rocks were early favorites, most anglers today use some kind of "synthetic rock" made of lead. These heavy orbs, cubes, triangles, or pencil weights are called sinkers, for obvious reasons. Their varied shapes and sizes allow them to be used in a variety of situations.

Probably the most commonly used sinkers are split shot, light pieces of lead (often shaped like small balls) that are crimped onto the line and used when casting light lines and small baits. The shot helps in casting, makes a very small splash when hitting the water, and will slowly sink the bait to the bottom. Split shot comes in a variety of sizes, and is commonly used when fishing for trout and other spooky fish who require a delicate presentation.

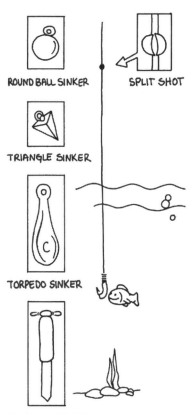

Larger sinkers are used for other purposes. When an angler wants to keep the bait on the bottom in areas disturbed by a lot of wave action, current, or tidal flow—triangle sinkers are preferred. This shape is available in a variety of weights and holds well on the bottom.

When you are fishing from a boat and want to fish just off the bottom, bouncing your bait without getting it caught in the rocks, a round ball is preferred. The ball will have less of a tendency to get stuck than a flatter shape. If you want to troll a bait down deep and need a sinker to help, "torpedo" or other streamlined shapes are available.

When drift fishing for salmon and steelhead, a popular weight is lead wire. This is sold in spools and varies in diameter, with $1/4$ or $3/16$ inch thickness most common. A length of wire is cut off according to the amount of weight required. Most often, this is about the size of a partly used pencil, and is thus often referred to as a pencil weight. It is attached to the line by a rubber cinch and swivel. The length of weight used should be just sufficient to allow the current to bounce the outfit along the bottom.

One point to remember when you have young'uns in tow is that lead tastes good to little kids but is one heck of a poison. Keep track of the sinkers, and don't let the little ones bite or mouth split shot or pencil lead.

When no stones are available for skipping and just plain chucking—chunks of lead are really tempting substitutes. When my boy, Steven, was five years old, I took him on a trip for steelhead with a newspaper editor. After one rather difficult climb to a lovely hole, I heard a splash as we were assembling our outfits. As we soon discovered, Steven had tossed our only coil of wire weight right into the middle of the pool. We had to pack up and head home!

Tools for the Tackle Box

Every tackle box should have a pair of needle nose pliers in it. These can be used for everything from extracting hooks and crimping on sinkers to opening pop bottles. A hook file or whetstone is essential for keeping hooks in condition, and, if you don't carry a pocket knife, at least have one in the tackle box. Knives with scissors are mighty handy for carving through world-class bird nests of monofilament. Don't forget to pack your fishing license and a set of current regulations. These change so often that there is just no getting on without them (said the judge).

6
Bait:
Snacks For Fish

Worms, Salmon Eggs, Bugs,
Minnows, and Other Odd Tidbits

Bill Wagner

In my experience, the highlight of a fishing trip for most really young anglers revolves not around the fish, but around the bait! Many of my own fondest memories of early trips are when Grandpa took us to the bait shop. The shop doubled as a bar and pool hall, and I can vividly recall the sawdust on the floor. Grandpa would have a beer, and I'd have a Nehi, as we waited for the bartender to put a couple of long dead sardines in a shoebox full of ice and pine shavings.

The main attraction of the shop was a murky tank full of live minnows. While we rarely pursued the larger game fish that required such bait, a few minutes of watching and searching for the biggest minnow in the tank always got me in the fishing mood!

Choosing Baits

When selecting bait, it is helpful to have some idea of what the fish you are going after like to eat. (Usually, there is no shortage of anglers willing to give you advice.)

Fishing with Small Fry

In general, most fish eat anything smaller than they are. Most are carnivores, although a few, such as carp, will eat vegetable matter as well.

Worms

The most popular bait for freshwater fish would have to be the common earthworm. Averaging about three inches in length, these fat pink beauties are considered the premier bait throughout most of America. Not only are they effective for catching everything from sturgeon and salmon to bluegill and trout, but they are readily available, harmless, and tough on a hook.

I have to admit that prior to the arrival of my youngsters, I hadn't baited up a worm in years. Most of my fishing was done with flies or other artificials. Getting back to the basics proved, however, to be one of my better moves. Not only did we catch a lot of fish, but the kids had a great time with the bait!

When I was a kid, collecting the worms was a fascinating ritual. Grandpa would grumble that the worm crop had been really poor that year, and we'd grab a shovel and head for the garden. Very carefully he'd dig up the loose soil around the tomatoes. My job was to break up the clods and secure the worms. We'd put the little crawlers in a jar of loose soil for our trip to the river or pond, and would carefully return any unused wrigglers to their home under the tomatoes at the end of the day.

Fortunately, earthworms are available almost everywhere. I can always find a couple of dozen underneath my dandelion patch on the hill next to the house. I just pull up a plant and find a few worms at each stem. There are those who claim rototilling builds character in a worm.

If I need a lot of worms, I'll make a late night stalk at a pioneer cemetery down the block. On wet nights, the worms will come out of their holes and munch on the cut grass. If you walk softly, you can grab them before they return to their lairs. We always use a flashlight with a red lens for the effort. White light will scare the critters, but red seems to have little effect.

For those strange folks who don't relish midnight trips to the graveyard or city park, there are commercial liquids now available that will bring subterranean worms up to the surface. These mixtures are not toxic to worms or people, but they do make life unpleasant enough for the worms, who pop up to the surface post haste. There are also electrical devices available that produce enough current in the ground to bring worms to the surface, but that's getting a little too hi-tech for me. People have fried themselves with these gadgets, so don't let the kids use them.

If you don't want to get your hands dirty (a trait which will not serve you well as a fisherman), you can always

Taryn Howe
age 11

buy your worms for a buck a dozen or so at a local bait shop or sporting goods department. Worms are easy to raise and breed, and a flourishing industry has developed around them.

However you secure your worms, they will have a magnetic effect on young anglers. There is something irresistible about digging in the dirt and pulling out the writhing contents. Some of the big "snakes" (worms can reach a foot in length) can spook little ones, but pretty soon they develop a friendship with the pink lengths of bait.

One good thing about worms is that they are safe. Being vegetarians with no teeth, stingers, or other bad habits, they will not harm little fingers, toes, or noses. Even if the kids get so curious or bored that they actually try to gross out their elders by eating (or enticing the baby to eat) a worm or two, there is no danger involved. Worms are great foodstuff, rich in protein and low in cholesterol!

The best thing about worms, however, is that they make great bait. If I'm fishing a new lake or pond, I almost always bring along a carton of worms. There are virtually no gamefish around that won't be tempted by a fat nightcrawler. Worms can be fished under a bobber to attract panfish or bass, and can be fished on the bottom to tempt catfish or carp. Unlike most other baits, worms are tough and durable. Fish may chew the bait off, but a well hooked worm will stay on a long time.

The best way to impale a worm is to thread it on the hook. Special worm hooks with small curved areas and long shafts are best for this effort. Don't just poke the hook through a worm's length in a couple of places. If a fish can bite a dangling section of worm without taking the hook, it'll easily pull the worm off the hook. Stick the point of the hook in one end of the worm, and thread the rest on the hook. Any excess worm should be removed.

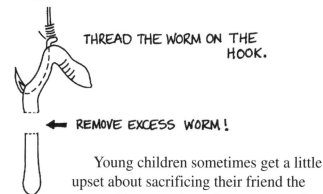

THREAD THE WORM ON THE HOOK.

◄— REMOVE EXCESS WORM!

Young children sometimes get a little upset about sacrificing their friend the worm. Cartoons show the worm standing on the hook enticing the fish; actually sticking the little critter is another thing. My youngsters tend to be rather sadistic by nature (a trait passed on from their mother!), and would love to stomp and tear the worms if that were permitted. So the threading of the worm is a curiosity rather than a tragedy in our family. If your children are a tad more sensitive, a little explanation of the procedure may be required.

A properly threaded worm is a great bait to use with small fry. Not only is it popular with the fish, but it is a tough, long lasting bait that will usually stay on the hook until something tries to bite it off. This gives you time to work on another child's outfit out while the first is still in the water!

While earthworms or nightcrawlers are the most popular worm used in fishing, several other varieties are available. Many trout fishing areas sell red worms. These worms are small and more brilliantly colored than nightcrawlers, which seems to make them mighty attractive to fish. Their small size requires the use of smaller hooks.

In the realm of the worm are a number of look-alikes that work very well for enticing small fish. If you do much panfishing, you'll probably have the opportunity to use meal worms or maggots as bait. These little critters are the larval stages of various flying critters and make tasty morsels when baited on a tiny hook. While the thought of putting a maggot on a hook may turn you off, the reality isn't all that bad.

These little larvae are neither slimy nor likely to chomp or sting. Kids love to dig around and find the "mini-worms," and they are easy to hook. With their shorter length, they don't require as complicated a threading as do larger worms, so a kid can practice the hooking procedure. Small hooks are best for baiting, and they will penetrate a lot less deeply if they hit little hands by mistake. If you are doing the hooking, and using tiny hooks, you might want to leave the barb in place. A lot of bait action can work a mealworm right off the hook.

A final worm worthy of mention is commonly called a pile worm. These foot long monsters are commonly used as bait in San Francisco Bay and other west coast areas. Looking much like a salt water centipede, they are favorites for striped bass, flounder, and various types of sea perch. They do, however have one major drawback. On the head of these worms are enormous pincers that absolutely petrify me!

I'm really not sure how hard a pileworm can chomp, but I've always taken major precautions. Before baiting a pileworm, I'll either put on gloves or cut off its head! This

bait, unlike earthworms or larva, falls apart in segments
pretty easily. I've had the most success when I thread it as
far as possible on a long shanked hook. It certainly attracts
a lot of fish, but it is so tender on the hook that it doesn't
last long. In fact, it usually causes more excitement in the
bait box than in the water!

Salmon Eggs

A very popular bait for salmon and trout are salmon
eggs. These eggs are available in clusters (taken from fish
when the connecting membrane is still intact) or in single
eggs (usually preserved and packed in little jars with oil).
Why salmon will eat eggs from their own species is open
to conjecture, but my guess is that most fish will eat any

Tasnim Schatz
age 8

fish eggs they run into.
Clustered eggs are usually
cut into nickel sized pieces and
held onto a hook by a loop tied
to the eye, or are wrapped in a
piece of cheese cloth or nylon to
hold the glob of eggs together.
Single eggs are usually fished
on a small hook designed especially for that purpose and fitting cleanly inside the egg. Eggs
are dyed all colors, but I prefer the bright red
(which is closest to natural). Finicky trout will often have
very specific preferences, so it's best to ask a local angler
before you buy a jar.

In fact, talk to local anglers about the most effective
baits every chance you get. They'll be glad to share tips
with you. Anglers of every fishery and every water have

"secrets" (tactics as well as baits) that have proven to be particularly effective time after time. Send your kids over to question the most successful angler on the stream. I'll guarantee you'll have all the tips you can handle!

Jamie Brickell
age 10

Bugs and Other Crawly Things

A number of insects make good bait in fresh water. Grasshoppers and crickets are popular for most species of trout and panfish. Plentiful and common throughout the U.S., they are durable and safe for little hands. A small hook slipped carefully through the tough "armor" on the top of the insect will increase their lifespan in the water. The longer they keep moving, the more interest they attract.

Other bugs are unique to a particular area. As a general rule, bugs that are common food for the fish work well. If you are on a river during a hatch of salmon flies, for example, the

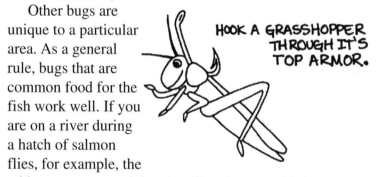

HOOK A GRASSHOPPER THROUGH IT'S TOP ARMOR.

odds are pretty good that they'll make a good bait.

One of my early successful efforts at hunting my own bait happened during a trip with my Grandpa to one of the alpine lakes in the Sierra Nevada mountains. The trout weren't doing much with our salmon eggs, so Grandpa suggested that I look for some dragonfly nymphs. These nasty looking critters were found in the lake on the aquatic

NYMPHS MAKE GOOD BAIT

STONEFLY NYMPH   **DRAGONFLY NYMPH**

CADDIS LARVA

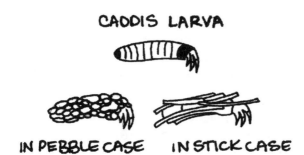

IN PEBBLE CASE   IN STICK CASE

weeds that grew near shore. I managed to hunt down a couple and was amazed at the result. As soon as the nymphs were cast into the deeper parts of the lake, they were sucked down by big rainbows.

Unfortunately, most of the nymphs had already hatched and were flying around the lake eating mosquitoes (what a great insect!). There were, however, a lot of their old "shells" left clinging to the weeds. I got a little bored and baited up one of the ectoskeletons. Whamo, the trout hit it as readily as they did one that was still filled with the live bug! I quickly caught my limit and was sold on the value of matching the hatch.

Minnows

As a general rule, big fish always eat smaller fish. With that in mind, one can see the value of small fish as bait for their larger cousins. The type of small fish used for bait, of course, depends on what you are after. Certain fish, in certain waters, prefer certain baitfish. In many freshwater lakes and rivers, these fish are referred to as minnows.

"Minnow" is a generic term used to describe dozens of different varieties of freshwater baitfish from shad to suckers. Most are small, rather undistinguished fish with shiny sides. They travel in large schools, making them popular foodstuff for larger fish and easily collected for bait sales.

Be aware, however, that live minnows are only allowed in certain bodies of water. In many lakes and reservoirs, only dead minnows are legal bait. This is because minnows that escape can quickly overpopulate a lake, depriving the natural population of food and habitat. Be sure to check your angling regulations before filling up the minnow bucket.

Tasnim Schatz
age 8

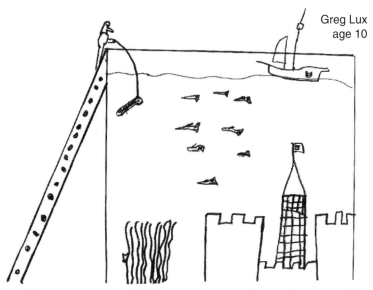

Greg Lux
age 10

Minnows are available at most bait shops. The tiny fish are kept in large tanks, well supplied with a good source of aerated water. Fishermen who use minnows usually have a minnow bucket, a large container that will hold enough water to keep the fish alive during the trip. The bait store will net the fish (or better yet, let the kids net them!), put them in your bucket, and charge a certain amount per fish.

Folks who use live bait often have live bait wells on their boats. These are more or less ornate containers that provide a good source of water for the fish. They usually have a mechanism for circulating air through the water, allowing them to keep the fish alive for an extended period of time. It is important that the fish be alive and healthy, since their swimming action is the key to their success as a bait.

There are a number of ways to fish live minnows. The most common ways of hooking the little fish are through the lips, and through the skin just forward of the dorsal fin. Gentle insertion of the hook should insure that the fish is not gravely injured and will continue to swim about, creating a commotion that entices something bigger to chomp it. A live minnow can be fished without any other tackle on the line, with a sinker if you want to get it down to a certain depth, or under a bobber if you want to fish it shallow and be able to watch all the action.

Live bait fishing requires quite a bit of attention to your gear and may be unsuitable for fishing with very young anglers. When the action is fast, kids will have a ball watching the bobber move in little circles when pulled by the minnow and then explode when pulled under by a big fish. Anglers of all sizes get a kick out of looking into the minnow bucket or tank.

Live baits are a favorite for saltwater and Great Lakes use. While the species of baitfish may vary from alewives to anchovies, the techniques for fishing them are similar to that employed in smaller bodies of water. Fish are kept alive in wells. The baitfish is hooked through the lips or back and is lowered (with sinker attached) to an effective depth. Larger fish, (from marlin to tuna to salmon) will readily chomp on their preferred diet.

During my first, (and only) outing for albacore tuna, the anchovy bait tank provided the sole excitement of our trip. In some twenty hours of boat ride and fishing, we only landed three fish for a thirty man charter. Between bouts of seasickness, I had a great time netting and playing with the little fish in the mid-boat enclosure. By the time we released the tiny fish at the end of the trip—very few had been called into action—I had become pretty good friends with most of them.

Bait: Snacks for Fish

In saltwater angling, use of all or part of a dead baitfish is more common than baiting with live minnows. Live baitfish require a lot of attention to keep them that way. One has to catch and transfer them carefully and keep them in a suitable habitat until used for fishing. Most baitfish purchased have been frozen to be sold at a later date.

Frozen baitfish are more convenient, but it is still a good idea to keep them in as good a shape as possible. While a number of gamefish could care less about the looks of the bait, those who feed primarily by sight are much more likely to take a bait that looks like it was alive sometime in the same decade! If you are fishing for one of those species, select a bait that has all of its scales intact and is not discolored.

Most dead bait is frozen for sale, but you can also find baitfish or baitfish parts packed in oil or even salted. During one rather interesting fishing trip to Southern California, the charterboat provided buckets of anchovies dehydrated in rocksalt. The shriveled up little fish looked none too appetizing, but the bottom fish seemed to like them fine. Salted anchovy did have one great benefit. They were as tough as leather, while frozen or even fresh anchovy is pretty mushy stuff for keeping on the hook. Salmon or other more persnickety feeders would have been hard to fool, but rockfish will bite most anything!

My kids love to cut up the bait. I always take along a rather dull knife for the effort. When we are out fishing for sturgeon or flounder, the "quality" of the slices is of little concern, and the kids will work diligently preparing enough chunks for our outing.

Tasnim Schatz
age 8

Other Saltwater Baits

Saltwater anglers have a particularly wide choice of effective baits. An excellent choice for most saltwater fishing is squid. Not only is it one of the toughest baits (it will stay on a hook for hours), but everything likes it. Squid are found throughout the ocean, have no natural defenses save a little speed and ink, and are great fish food. I've caught everything from perch to shark on squid and will use it whenever I get a chance.

Shrimp, both alive and dead, are also good saltwater fare. Most species of saltwater fish have occasion to feast on the huge schools of shrimp that share their habitat. In

Christopher Noel
age 11

addition to garden variety shrimp, their are species unique to different locales. San Francisco Bay features a special little shrimp, called a grass shrimp, that is excellent for both sturgeon and bass, and also serves well for flounder and perch.

In the Northwest, a popular bait for salmon, flounder, perch, and almost anything else is a critter that goes under the several names of ghost, mud, or sand shrimp. Collected from its muddy bay hole, this soft crustacean is a real winner at the end of a line. It does, however, have several drawbacks as a bait. First, it is extremely fragile, dying if it gets too warm, too dry, too crowded, or if you just look at if funny. As soon as it dies, it turns to mush and is impossible to keep on the hook, stinks to high heaven, and poisons all the other shrimp in the container!

In addition to it's fragile nature, the darn thing is also a menace. While all of its body is soft and squishy, it does boast a huge claw that puts a crawdad to shame! Grab casually into the bait box and you are likely to get a significant pinch. On a day when your fingers are frozen anyway, one more owie is no fun. The kids, needless to say, just love the shrimp and will poke away at them for hours.

On much of the West Coast, many varieties of shrimp and sand crabs can be found by digging under kelp washed up on the beach. Finding and collecting these little crustaceans is easy enough even for little ones, and makes a good adventure. Fished in the surf or off the rocks, they are excellent not only for snaring a few fish, but for teaching the kids a little bit about the food chain.

Mussels are found on most rocks and have an orange meat that makes great bait. Clams work well too.

Other Freshwater Baits

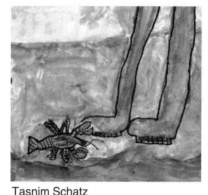

Tasnim Schatz
age 8

Freshwater anglers use many different natural baits to tempt fish to hook. One good thing to remember when using any sort of tough skinned bait is to have the hook protruding enough that it will penetrate the fish when the hook is set. If you bury the hook too deeply in a tough bait, a strike will not have enough force to drive the hook into the fish.

Many streams and lakes harbor a feisty crustacean that can serve as excellent bait. Crayfish, or crawdads, are tasty fare for both human and finny predators. Looking much like little lobsters, they have been successfully used to catch bass, trout, sturgeon and most other gamefish. They can be stored in any moist container, and they last forever on a hook. While kids love to play with them, crawdads do have a good pair of pincers that will cause major discomfort when they get a grip on a small pair of fingers. As children get older, they can be taught the proper way to handle crawdads and other critters with pincers. Gripped securely just behind their pincers, crawdads can be safely handled and baited.

Some freshwater rivers have clams that are excellent for perch and catfish.

Catfish have inspired an awful collection of baits. While I'm partial to using worms or chunks of baitfish for the feisty bottom feeders, all kinds of special stinkbaits are manufactured or homemade for use in catching Old Whiskers. Most ingredients feature some kind of fish or fish parts, cheese, blood of something, and a doughy filler. Folks also like to use chicken livers, and guts, and most any other awful stuff they can find. Catfish are, for the most part, scavengers, and they do feed primarily by smell, so a little odor will help. I have a limit to the amount that I can tolerate, but that is a matter of preference!

Those who chase after carp roll up dough balls for use in that fishery. Carp are large fish and are available in almost all large or small bodies of fresh water. A European import, the big fish feed primarily on vegetable matter and a few insects. With that preference in mind, bread is not a bad choice. Most any mixture that will produce a dough tough enough to hold on a hook for a few minutes will do. I've had pretty good luck with a mixture of week-old bread and water. The fish like it fine, but it doesn't hold on too well. Make up your own stiff dough and give it a try. Carp aren't picky and provide a real battle for a young angler.

Bass fishermen are partial to frogs and water snakes. Hooked lightly below the skin, these baits provide a lot of movement and are popular items on the fish's natural menu. Mice and baby ducklings are also effective for catching bass and very large brown trout, but even most grown-ups shy away from sacrificing cute little critters as bait when there are imitations that work just fine!

Strange Stuff

There are, I am ashamed to admit, a good number of baits that have no business being used for anything— except that they work! For the life of me I can't figure out why native trout in pristine high country lakes will go bananas over a wad of Velveeta™ cheese formed into a ball around the hook, but they do. There isn't a cow within a thousand miles, but the stupid fish (the same ones who ignore your carefully tied flies) will chomp on the orange goo as if they were accustomed to schools of cheese bits swimming by. If the fishing slows, you can always spread your "bait" on some crackers and have a snack with the kids.

Tony Charon
age 11

Another bait that works great for trout are marshmallows. Most popular are the varieties that are small enough to fit easily on a hook. Commercial interests have put them in jars, dyed and flavored. But a bag of regular mini-mallows sold for human consumption works just as well and can double as a treat for the anglers! Fish sandwiches, made by layering salmon eggs between marshmallows, work very well in most trout lakes. The marshmallow floats the egg just above the bottom, and the whole mess is just too much for a trout with a sweet tooth to resist.

With baits like these it is easy to understand why some people will believe that most anything can catch fish. I still get a chuckle when I think back on a conversation I had with a youngster many years ago. In the best tradition, this precocious angler had observed us catching fish while he and his mother were having no luck. The five year old came marching up to me and asked what we were using for bait. I told him, honestly, that we were catching our trout on salmon eggs and worms.

After a little small talk and a long look at our catch, the tiny angler went back to mama with the news. My wife happened to be walking past the boy as he was giving his intelligence report to his mom. "What in the world did you tell that little boy?" my irate wife asked. Somewhat surprised at her attitude, I meekly replied that I had told him we were using salmon eggs and worms. My wife broke into a wide grin. "That little kid has his mother going after 'ham and eggs' to use with their worms." What the heck, maybe it worked!

Cindi Moore
age 10

Abigail Maxfield
age 9

7
Spinners, Spoons, and Other Phony Food

Lures, Flies, Plastic and Polymer Imitations

Bill Wagner

Thousands of years ago, some perceptive Neanderthal noticed that the fish in the neighborhood pond would become so hungry they'd bite at the tips of hanging branches, falling leaves, or most anything that touched the water. Early angler may have grabbed a short branch and wiggled the tip in the waters. As a fish rose to bite the woody tidbit, it was promptly clubbed and dragged triumphantly home for dinner.

From these early beginnings, mankind learned that it could attract fish with something other that real fish food. As the fish in the pond became more "club shy," increasingly attractive artificials were developed. Perhaps some weeds or flowers were tied to a length of vine, or a snip of fur and feathers the same color as a local insect, or a bit of carved wood that wiggled enticingly and lured fish within range of spear or club.

With the development of the fish hook, sophisticated lures were created and techniques were refined and perfected.

Scott Mahe
age 11

- 69 -

A few millennia later, we have a whole industry devoted to the creation of a wide variety of lures, plugs, flies, and poppers that will bring the choosiest fish to hook.

Hardware

One of the most popular and easy to fish of the modern lures is the spinner. While this lure is unlike any actual food species, its motion in the water is irresistible to most fish. It consists of a hook (with one to three points) and a blade—a chunk of beaten or shaped metal that spins wildly when dragged through the water. Spinners are available in a variety of colors to suit the preference of any angler or fish (not always the same!).

Spinners are easily set in motion. One need only cast them out and reel in the line (a good spinner will revolve regardless of the speed). A healthy current will activate the spinner even without retrieval. A spinner can be trolled behind a boat. Spinners have pretty good weight to them, but in particularly fast or deep water (when you are after species that frequent the deeper holes in the stream), you may want to add a little weight above the spinner to bring it down to fish level.

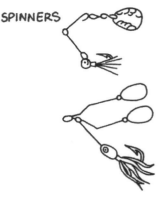

SPINNERS

SPOONS

Also popular and easy to use is a metal lure called a spoon. Of ancient design, spoons are shaped something like a baitfish and imitate a minnow's natural wiggling or swimming motion when activated by retrieval or current. Spoons have a small hole near the front and, often, a tiny swivel that prevents the line from becoming twisted by the lure's motion. Trailing the lure is a hook designed to catch the fish as it bites the spoon.

Many mail order companies sell the components for making spinners. Any child old enough to fish with a spinner can learn to make his or her own lures. These home-made treasures will be a lot cheaper, work just as well, and add another element of interest to the endeavor. Spend the cold days of winter working with your kids on the lures for spring and summer.

Spoons can be cast and retrieved in the same manner as spinners. Since spoons are often heavier than spinners, they are easier to cast and will fish a little deeper in fast moving waters. Because their motion is easy to activate, they are also good for jigging near the bottom. To jig, lower the lure to the bottom, then raise it slightly by lifting the rod tip, and allow it to flutter back toward the bottom. This motion is effective in attracting all kinds of bottom feeding fish, from ling cod to salmon.

Plugs are among the most attractive of artificial lures. Originally carved from wood and painted to enhance their realism, they are meticulously designed to look like bait—such as frogs, mice, and various kinds of minnows. Today's plugs are made of both wood and plastic. They may consist of one or several pieces, and are engineered to work on the surface, or to dive and bump along the bottom.

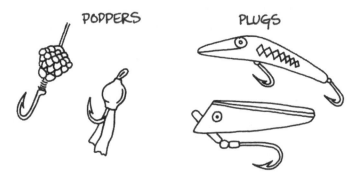

POPPERS   PLUGS

Hooks may be arranged on the underside, or the rear, or both. They can be fished by casting and retrieving, or by trolling. Because of their durability, plugs have always been a favorite. Old plugs, having survived years of battle with fish and snag, are now collector items, valued at hundreds of dollars apiece!

My grandfather left me a good number of old wooden lures that he used to fish the waters of his native Wisconsin. These bass and musky plugs are now on display in my den and are one of my treasured possessions. You might consider taking your kids to a few garage sales to collect their own antique fishing tackle. Not only will they learn a little about fishing, but they well have a lot of fun searching for angling treasures.

Flies

The most imaginative artificial lure is the fly. An angling favorite for hundreds of years, flies are made of feathers, cloth, fur, and a variety of other materials tied directly onto a hook. These creations look, more or less, like some form of insect, amphibian, mammal, or other fish food.

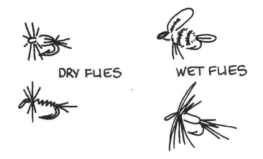

DRY FLIES   WET FLIES

The art of tying and effectively using such lures is extremely popular world wide and has led to the founding of many local, national, and international clubs. Fly tyers and fishers gather to share fly tying ideas, to extoll the pleasures of their sport, and (in these environmentally troubled times) to discuss ways to preserve the waters where they can pursue their passion.

Ready-tied flies are sold at general sporting goods stores and, in wonderful variety, at shops specializing in fly fishing. Instructions for tying flies are available in books and magazines, and through classes sponsored by fly shops, community centers, and fishing clubs. Some outdoor shows offer the opportunity for youngsters to sit down at a well-stocked fly bench and make their own creations under the guidance of experts. Nine and ten year olds with modest dexterity and patience can easily master fly tying basics. If you already have your own supply of fly tying materials, you may have observed that they are fascinating to the young (especially the new synthetic shiny and iridescent threads). With a little help, kids can tie up some imaginative creations that just might fool an innocent on your next excursion.

Fishing with Small Fry

As with other fishing clubs, local fly angling organizations welcome new members, especially young ones. They will gladly give you and your kids tips on fly fishing and tackle. After a winter of tying flies and telling lies, most clubs will schedule field trips where you and your kids can learn to fly fish from anglers with years of experience.

Flies can be fished in a variety of ways. They can be cast and retrieved, cast and drifted, jigged, or trolled. The motion and technique of choice depends on the type of fly used and the habits of the particular fish pursued. The impressive looking fly cast isn't always necessary or appropriate. You might let your youngster try just dangling an imitation over a likely looking undercut bank. Imitations of bugs such as grasshoppers and ants often work well here, and the kids will enjoy the element of stealth needed to sneak up on their prey.

Other Imitations

Arnold Reed
age 11

Many other lures are also available. A bass tackle box is generally full of realistically wiggly plastic worms in a variety of colors as well as frogs, salamanders, snakes and all sorts of other bait imitations made of molded polymers. Cork poppers work for both panfish and bass.

For ocean fishing, squid imitations consist of a thin sheath of plastic for a body and a hula skirt tattering for tentacles. Other lures and jigs may be nothing more than a snippet of yarn tied to a weighted hook. Any bit of color or shape seems to appeal to some species of bottom fish, who consider anything floating or moving and smaller than they to be fair game!

Artificial lures are used alone or in combination with one another and/or with bait. The list of available lures grows daily, fed by the imagination of anglers and lure manufacturers, and by the availability of new and inspiring materials. A basic tenant of the industry has long been that a good lure must at least catch a buyer in the tackle shop. You can now find electronic lures with flashing lights and sound. I draw the line at changing batteries in my lures.

Wendy Jackson
age 9

Fishing with Small Fry

Abigail Maxfield
age 9

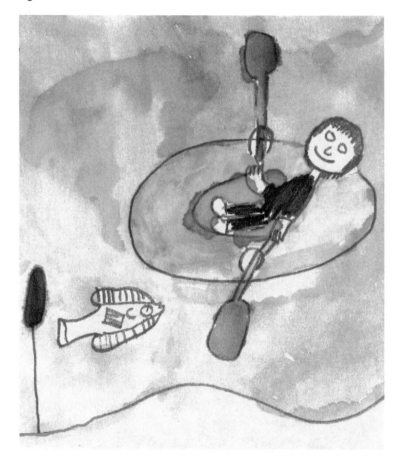

8
How To Find 'em

Identifying Places Where
Fish Like to Hang Out

Bill Wagner

Picking a good spot to fish is one of the challenges of fishing, even for veteran anglers. As a general rule, fish tend to frequent areas that offer food and protection. In both lakes and rivers, that usually means places that have some kind of natural or man-made "structure." Structure may be anything in the water other than water itself. Look for fish around big rocks, sunken trees, aquatic vegetation, bridge footings, and pier pilings. Underwater ledges and undercut banks also attract fish, offering cover for both fish and the creatures they prey upon naturally.

On one of my first outings with my oldest son, we hoped to catch a few fish from a popular pier on one of our local lakes. At first we tried emulating the other fishermen there. It is a fact that anglers inevitably seem to cast as far as gear and expertise will allow. You'll see those in boats casting toward shore, while others on shoreline fire toward the depths! But on this day, all of us were coming up fishless. Our bobbers bobbed undisturbed in the clear water near the middle of the lake.

Fishing with Small Fry

Reverting to previous experiences on a pier, I decided to try closer to home. I dropped our worm and bobber right next to a pier piling. Within seconds the little red and white plastic orb quivered and disappeared under the surface. Steven was overjoyed as we hauled in our first perch. We had the fun of catching and releasing dozens of little fish that day, but would have come home empty if we hadn't looked for the only structure available, the pier.

Small fish hide from larger fish, and the larger fish know where to look for them. If you look for structure in the water, you'll likely find fish of all sizes. Experienced tournament anglers use five figure boats and four figure electronics to look for structure under water. The rule holds for everyone, veteran and beginner: structure means fish. It also, unfortunately, usually means that you'll loose some gear to snags in the process, so always take along plenty!

"HIDE AND SEEK"

On big, slow moving waters, finding the best spot from shore can be tough. On big rivers like the Columbia, the Sacramento, the Mississippi, or any other body of water over a hundred feet across and murky—finding fish tends to be pretty random. Big rivers that flow through well-populated areas do have one advantage, however. They have been fished for hundreds of years, and a great deal of local knowledge is available. Anglers might be a little secretive about their favorite tiny pool in a hidden stream, but most consider really big bodies of water public domain and will be happy to give you help, especially if you have a couple of kids in tow.

Unlike big waters, small streams can be read on the spot to determine likely fishing holes. Even tiny fish in tiny creeks seek protection and food, and can be found near miniature versions of the structure you would look for in bigger waters: trailing branches from streamside brush, submerged roots, logs, and rocks, and undercut banks. Though the fish in the smallest streams may be well under legal keeper size, little streams can be a flowing aquarium for your youngsters to learn about fish habits and habitat.

Fish will often be waiting in the downstream part of a deep pool, where they have protection from predators and a good view of any food that happens to flow by. In most places on a stream, the fish will swim in place facing upstream. It is a good idea for you to walk and cast upstream, so that the fish don't see you coming.

Fish that grow up in a stream have learned to duck for cover at the first sign of a heron, raccoon, or human approaching their waters, so keep a low profile and you'll have the best luck. (Your little buddies may have the advantage here!) If the stream is murky, or the weather is overcast, you don't need to be as sneaky, but if the water is low and clear and the sun is high, it's best to hide your shape and shadow as much as possible.

Very young children will have trouble developing the skills necessary to fish some small streams, but most waters will have a few nice deep pools that can be easily fished from shore. Drift a worm or salmon egg into the depths, and the odds are pretty good that something will happen. Early morning and evening are usually your best times when weather is fair. Though fish feed throughout the day, they are less cautious when they are better hidden by the low light of morning and by late afternoon shadows.

◄ UPSTREAM

FISH ALWAYS HOLD THEIR HEADS UPSTREAM.

Ocean fishing can be fun given good weather and calm seas, but fishing from the shore (whether surf casting or fishing from the rocks) is too dangerous and requires too much skill for most anglers under ten. As children get a little older, those spots offer a lot of action and appeal. Rocky areas with a lot of tidepools can provide excellent fishing.

Our family had a favorite spot on a beach near Hearst Castle in central California where we had great fishing. We'd dig sand fleas from under the beach kelp and pry muscles off the rocks and would be set for bait. There was a really nice pool in a rocky formation out in the surf that was home to hundreds of hungry perch. Some were rainbow colored, some striped, others were speckled, and all offered terrific action and fine eating. But rocks and surf also offer clear and present dangers to youngsters who aren't old enough to use good fishing skills and common sense.

Surf fishing is also a lot of fun. Anglers use long rods and good casting reels to throw a bait or lure well out into the surf. Most wade at least thigh deep while casting. While catching a fish in the pounding surf is a great thrill, there are obvious dangers. In some locations, a parent can cast and bring the rod back to dry sand for the youngsters to fish. Obviously, it is necessary to pay careful attention to the children when on the beach. A couple of adults— one to cast, one to supervise—are in order.

Fishing a bay from a boat or pier is about as close to a sure thing as one can find. What you catch may not be edible, but that matters little to kids. Ask at local bait-shops for the best places, and which tides to fish them on.

Fishing with Small Fry

After some four decades of fishing, I still am quite predisposed to being skunked, a popular term for catching nothing! If you've never been skunked, you haven't fished much. But it is frustrating to be fishless when others are catching all kinds of critters. First time anglers, and those trying new waters, should freely quiz those already on location for tips.

Molly Emmons
age 9

9
When In Doubt, Jerk!

How to Hook a Fish

Phil Bullock

So what do you do if (and this *will* eventually happen if you and the little ones keep at it) something actually bites your bait or lure? The object of this activity is to embed the hook inside the fish's mouth. Since there is a lot of give in the line and rod, a forceful motion is usually necessary to do the job. After you jerk, reel in a little line. You should feel the vibrations of the struggling fish in the rod itself.

Bobber fishing is pretty easy to read. If the bobber bounces or goes under, you are getting a bite. Reel in the line until you have removed all the slack between angler and bobber. Kids love to jerk the rod the moment they see the bobber go under. Usually there is too much slack between them and the bobber for this to have any effect on the fish. If, after the slack is removed, the bobber is still active, jerk the rod vigorously from horizontal to vertical position. If you don't feel a strumming on the end of the line, let the bobber sit for a minute or so, watching closely to see if it is still moving. If it goes down again, repeat the procedure (reel in slack, set the hook), and bring in the fish.

Fishing with Small Fry

If you are getting lots of bobber action but aren't hooking fish, chances are you are using too big a bait or too big a hook. Many anglers bait worms carelessly, allowing a fish to grab a dangling tidbit without hooking itself. Re-bait carefully and try again. If your hook is too big for the fish's mouth, the fish can easily avoid the sharp point while sampling or examining your offering. Try tying on a smaller hook. Some large fish (such as shad) have very small mouths. Match your hook to the size of the anticipated mouth, rather than to the size of the fish.

Fishing without a bobber, an angler must rely on signals communicated directly through the line and rod to notify of action below. A fishing rod is made of material that should transmit the feel of any action to the angler.

To acquaint your children with this feel before your first outing, play "going fishing" in the backyard or park. Give each child a chance to hold the rod with eyes closed. Take out about thirty feet of line, and make a series of

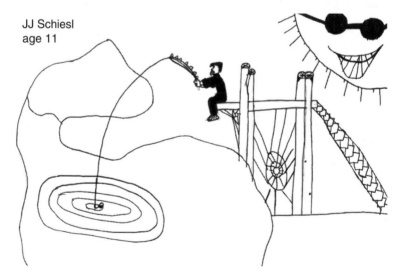

JJ Schiesl
age 11

sharp pulls. Have them open their eyes and watch for movement at the rod tip, and for movement of the line. (With a really sensitive rod, one can feel the vibrations when a person holds the taut line to their adams apple and speaks.)

When fish take a bait, they usually first give a series of little pulls. This is a tug-of-war effort against the counter-pull of the line and sinker. Sometimes this movement is very slight. Anglers call light pulls "nibbles." The nibbles become more violent as the fish realizes that something is not right and tries to swim away with its prize. This movement is called a bite. When fishing for most species, either a series of nibbles or a bite should be met with a hard jerk of the fishing rod. Experienced anglers hold the rod tip near the water when a nibble or bite is felt (or even while waiting for a bite). Learning to "keep the rod tip down" will be a challenge for most youngsters, as it is for most beginning anglers. When all slack is reeled in, the rod is jerked up to vertical position with a hard motion to set the hook. This motion, if applied when the fish has the bait in its mouth, will result in a solidly hooked fish. There are a few exceptions to the rule. A few fish will pull on a bait gently, avoiding the hook. To catch them, you will need to give them a little extra line before they really take it down. Other species (such as shad) have soft mouths that will rip if the hook is set too firmly. But in most cases, if you feel a nibble or a bite, set the hook with vigor, and you'll have a fish on!

If you are trolling, or retrieving a lure, a bite will usually be felt quite differently. When a fish goes after a moving object, especially one it thinks is alive, the strike will be much more noticeable. The rod tip will jerk violently, and your retrieve will halt suddenly. No subtle signals here. The fish may even hook itself. But in most cases, you will still need to strike with some force to embed the hook securely.

The take on a floating fly or surface lure may be altogether different again. Surface feeding fish may jump clear out of the water in pursuit of your offering. Or they may gently slurp down a fly, just barely breaking the surface. The only sign of the take may be the sudden appearance of a ring of disturbed water (called a rise), sometimes accompanied by a gentle "bloop!" Most children will need to learn to see a rise on the surface of the water. When insects are hatching and fish are feeding on the surface, you can make a game of counting the number of rises, or of finding the rise that goes with the "bloop!"

Alan Sanders
age 9

When fishing a fly upon the surface (called dry fly fishing), it is important for anglers to keep an eye on the fly at all times. (Fish are quick to recognize that a dry fly is not really a juicy bug.) Maintaining this level of concentration is very difficult for youngsters, but is essential for success. It's probably best to save serious fly fishing for later in their angling experience.

When in Doubt, Jerk!

If your fly, lure, or bait is working under water, it's a good idea to strike whenever the drift varies or feels unnatural. In Northwest and Great Lakes streams, anglers do a lot of drift fishing. A bait or lure with sinker attached is bounced along the bottom of the streambed with the drift of the current. Any time this motion stops, anglers set the hook. Watch the angle of the line at the point it enters the water. Any sudden change signals that the lure has stopped moving. A good deal of the time the sinker has merely caught a rock or root, but the motion of a fish taking the hook is so subtle that it feels exactly the same. Salmon and steelhead usually hold the bait lightly in their mouths at first. Since it's better to be safe than sorry—when in doubt, jerk!

Marie Rogers
age 8

Drift boat
Strong, metal
moving, banging, drifting,
bumping against slippery rocks
fishing boat

Fishing with Small Fry

Jenifer Whitcomb
age 9

10
Happy Landings

Playing and Landing Fish

Oregon Dept. of Fish and Wildlife

When a fish is hooked the fun really starts! In fact, the next stage of the game is referred to as playing the fish! Remember, the object is to have a good time, not to quickly horse some poor fish ashore. Landing a fish too quickly (still full of fight) can be hard on both angler and fish. The basic principle behind playing a fish is simple. Cold blooded critters, fish included, have a relatively small amount of blood in their bodies. As a result, they have limited oxygen capacity and tend to tire more quickly than warm blooded animals. This doesn't mean that they can't put up one heck of a fight! After all, they are streamlined, strong, and determined. But they can't keep it up as long as a mammal might.

For example, if you hook into a hundred pound sturgeon while fishing with thirty pound test, it might take you an hour or so to bring the fish to net. Hook a harbor seal of the same weight, and it'll run your line right off the spool! If you doubt the accuracy of my hypothesis, go out to a football field with your favorite German shepherd or lab. Tie thirty pound test line to its collar and have a buddy call the dog from the other end of the field. Either you tighten the line so tight that it breaks, or the dog takes it all off your spool.

Another advantage the angler has is that fish must also battle the water. In general, the fish has to fight the water to get away and (unlike the angler, who has terra firma to push against) has no friction to help it in its battle against the pressure applied by angler and line. Of course, in a rapid river or screaming tide the water flow may give the fish an edge.

You can further tire the fish by using the drag on the reel. With the drag properly set, the fish will need to exert extra effort to pull out line. As the fish tires, raise the rod tip to pull it in closer, and reel in the slack line. Lower the

Josh Moskowitz
age 9

rod tip for a few moments, and repeat the process. This pumping motion allows you to recover line and bring the fish in. If the fish swims away or runs out more line after taking a breather, let it go and enjoy the battle. If your equipment has been selected to handle the size fish you have hooked, you can be sure that the fish will eventually tire and allow itself to be landed.

The sound, look, and feel of a fish running out line is one of the joys of fishing. Even a little bluegill can set a reel spinning if the angler is using appropriately light gear. No doubt about it, though, the out-of-control feeling of a fish pulling out line will panic your young anglers. But it is a positive and manageable panic, and being there to talk your youngster through it is a darned satisfying experience for a parent! Resist the temptation to take over at this point, even if your youngster hands you the rod. Remind the kids that the point is to have fun, not to bring home meat. Whether the battle is won by angler or fish, the success is in fooling the fish to begin with, and in the fun of playing the fish as well as luck and skill allow.

With tackle that is well suited and properly adjusted, the kids will tire out the fish before it reaches the bank or boat. If they are using gear that is too heavy, they may be able to haul in a fish before it is tired. This greatly reduces the chances of a successful landing. Don't bring a fish in until it has quit struggling and has turned over on its side.

Kids dearly love to haul fish to shore. My youngster's favorite was to run up the beach dragging the fish behind him as he charged off into the brush! This method may be quick and exciting, but a lot of fish are lost in the effort, and there really are more sporting (if less invigorating) ways to bring in the catch.

On a pier or fishing platform, one usually just has to haul the fish up the side. If you have to land a fish in this manner, equip the kids with relatively heavy gear. Pulling a fish clear of the water puts a lot of strain on the rod and reel as well as hooks, line, and leader. Be extra sure the fish has tired itself out while in the water. A flailing fish will almost certainly pull itself free of the hook on the way up.

If the kids are lucky enough to catch a really big fish from a pier, there are ways to land it other than trying to horse it up. You can lower a crab ring and swing it under your fish. These rings are strong and will carry a lot of weight. During one cold November morning, I used a crab ring to retrieve a rather unlikely catch. Our three month old doberman puppy fell through some old planks and swam over to a piling, where it hung on for dear life. I lowered my crab ring near him and yelled for him to swim into the net. Miraculously, he actually climbed onto the mesh. Unfortunately, he was so heavy that I lost my grip when he was almost up to the deck, and he fell back into the water. But after that moment to more or less compose himself, he managed to swim to shore!

Another way you can help the youngsters bring a big fish up to the dock or deck is by lowering a large treble hook into the water and snagging the catch (snagging an already caught fish is legal; snagging a free swimming fish is illegal in most states). Finally, the angler can walk down the pier to the beach while pulling the fish along the water. On a really long pier, this will take some time and may cause a little inconvenience to others, but folks are usually glad to help—especially when the angler just measures up to their belt buckle.

Fishing from a beach, lake shore, or river bank usually involves pulling the fish up on dry land eventually (called beaching a fish). The kids will want to haul in the fish as soon as possible. But a fish that comes in full of fight can cause all kinds of problems in shallow water. Encourage the little ones to enjoy fighting the fish at a distance. Don't let a lot of slack form in the line between them and the fish. When the action slows, give the signal to start bringing the fish in.

Losing a fish on the beach is usually the result of two mistakes. The first is lifting the fish's head out of the water. When we want to pull a fish up on shore, the most natural method is to raise the rod high and lift the fish onto the beach. Unfortunately, when you get a fish into the air you lose the resistance of the water, and every twist and flop is magnified. One good shake of its head will free the fish from the hook. Have the kids keep the fish in the water by holding the rod tip about waist high as they reel in. The object is to keep the fish submerged until it is on the bank or close enough to grab, gaff, or net.

A second common mistake is allowing too much slack in the line. As the distance between angler and fish decreases, each

Emily Fabbry
age 10

movement of the fish is magnified. If, at this point, the angler drops the rod tip so that slack is created, the fish may sense the relaxation of tension and make a sudden move that can snap the line. The reel doesn't have time to feed line in this situation. Remind the angler to "keep the line tight," and bring the fish in slowly and carefully.

Sometimes you may have to improvise a little. When I was about ten, I was fishing with my brother in a favorite tide pool. We were catching a few little surf perch and having a great time. On one cast, however, things changed. I felt a hard bite and set the hook. Instead of dashing around wildly, this fish went down to the bottom and hung on. After a lot of panic and tugging, I finally brought the fish to the surface. Unlike the pretty little surf perch, this monster was big and ugly.

Josh Spenser
age 12

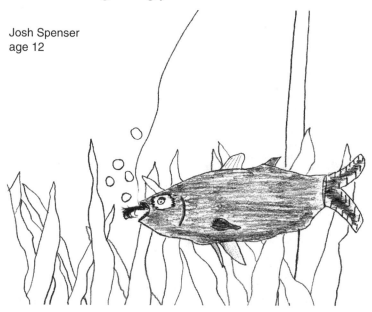

I had been hauling my catch up on the rocks, but even my twenty pound test would be at risk with this critter. After some thought, I guided the fish through a channel to a little sandy bottomed finger in the rocks. As the tide went out, the fish was stranded on the sand. Since my little brother was afraid to go after the fish, I had to do some coaxing to get him to jump onto the sand as the tide retreated. Fortunately, he was able to push the fish up to me and to scramble up the rocks before the next breaker hit! That twelve pound cabazon was a catch that neither of us will ever forget.

Using a net to land a fish is most essential if you are fishing where you would have to lift the fish with your line in order to bring it onto shore or into a boat. If you can avoid lifting a fish into the air, you will drastically increase your chances of a successful landing. Netting a fish is not a fool proof procedure, however, and a good number of fish are lost at this point.

Let your kids practice their netting skills on fish that are plentiful and easy to handle. The principles are the same whether the fish is a five inch bluegill or a twenty pound pike. Practice on the little fish that don't really matter, make a big deal over every success, and interject pointers as the opportunities allow.

The most important secret in netting is to be sure that a fish is good and tired when you try to land it. Anglers, especially little ones, want that fish in NOW! A "green" fish will cause all kinds of trouble. Play the fish until it tires, and you won't have to be an expert netter to land it.

Be sure that your net is the right size. Trying to net a fish with a net that is too small will insure disaster. If you can only get half the fish into the net, you had best consider other landing techniques! On the other hand, if you have a net that is so big that the fish can slip through the mesh, you're out of luck.

Many anglers like to net a fish from the head. While this technique works pretty well in ocean situations with plenty of water to work, I prefer netting from the tail end. Anything that you put near the hook can cause disaster. If you start with the head and the fish decides to battle, it can easily catch the hook in the net's mesh or frame and pull it loose. I approach a tired fish from the backside. Slip the net under the tail, bring it over the head, and lift. If the fish still has a lot of energy, it will slip out of the net, hook still firmly in place. Play the fish until it is tired, then try the net again.

Another tool sometimes used to land large gamefish is a gaff (a large hook attached to a stiff handle). A gaff can be thrust through a fish's mouth, slipped up the gill slits, or driven through its body. Gaffs are only used on large fish, ten pounds or better—specimens that are best left to anglers who carry a little more weight themselves! Gaffs are quite dangerous and should not be used by (or around) younger kids.

Dangerous and powerful fish such as large sharks or halibut are commonly shot before being hauled on board. There are, of course, a lot of dangers involved in firearms, and I certainly would avoid contact with anything large enough to require artillery when children are around. Some very large species, such as marlin, giant tuna and the like, are often harpooned, stuck with a flying gaff, or looped around the tail. These chores are best handled by very skilled captains and deck hands and are seldom common practice on Saturday outings with the munchkins!

Jessie Moreno
age 12

A common procedure for landing largemouth bass is to grab the fish's lower lip with thumb and forefinger. This usually immobilizes the fish and allows you to remove the hook easily. Younger children, however, seem inevitably to find a way to grab the hook in the process, so you are usually better off netting or beaching the fish.

Grabbing the sides of the fish can prove to be dangerous as well. Hooks can come out and catch little hands and arms. Fish don't have very good handles, so grabbing is not a recommended procedure.

In a pinch, a wide variety of "weapons" can be used to subdue a fish. I recall once going over the side with a catsup bottle to try to sedate a shark that was too large for our gaff. Hammers and wrenches from a tool chest work well in a pinch if the fish is too big and your net too small.

You may inadvertently catch something huge while fishing with the kids, but remember, whether a shark or a crappie, all fish should be played until they are pooped. Only a tired fish can be landed safely and effectively.

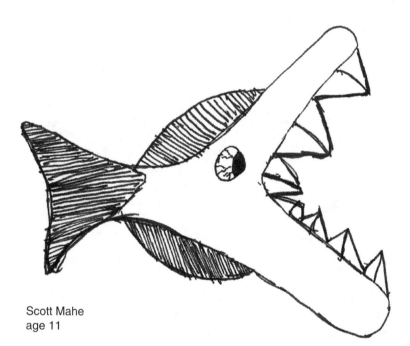

Scott Mahe
age 11

11
Off The Hook

How to Safely Unhook a Fish

Oregon Dept. of Fish and Wildlife

When the fish is successfully boated, netted, beached or otherwise landed, it's time to concentrate on hook removal. Hooks are sharp and hazardous and should be handled with caution. A sudden quick flip by a head or tail can drive a hook right into the hands, fingers, or other body parts of a young angler.

If you are going to keep your fish for eating, the easiest way to remove a hook is to pull it from a dead fish. A quick rap on the back of the fish's head with a heavy object (rock, tool handle, hammer) will do the trick. When in doubt, pop it a couple of times. The whacking may seem a bit sadistic, but a quick dispatch is far more humane than the prolonged suffocation the fish will otherwise suffer if left to die in the air.

Once the fish is dispatched, you should make sure that the line is slack. If a hook is pulled loose from a fish while the rod is still bent and the line is taut, the hook will fly violently through the air and may well end up in an ear, lip, or some equally undesirable location.

Fishing with Small Fry

Unbarbed hooks can usually be worked loose by pulling gently with the fingers. If the hook is embedded in tough skin or cartilage, needle nose pliers do a good job of getting the hook out. Special "hook out" tools are made for the purpose, but needle nose pliers are just fine.

If the hook is completely swallowed or stuck deep in a fish's gullet, you might want to just cut the line and retrieve the hook when you clean the fish. If you decide to take the line cutting route, leave a few inches sticking out of the mouth to remind you that the fish has a sharp spot inside.

Allison Wong
age 9

Always check your hook and the few inches of line above it after it is removed from the fish. It is pretty easy to bend a hook or knick a line in the course of prying the hook lose. Changing a hook or replacing a frayed leader will insure equal success on your next catch. It's also a good idea to test the hook for sharpness after each successful hook-up. To test a hook, run the point lightly over your thumbnail. If the point slides easily over your nail, it needs to be sharpened.

After a fish is landed, most kids will want to ogle, poke, and otherwise handle their catch. While this is O.K. with species such as trout, many fish have spines and stickers that can make nasty punctures in unwary fingers. Catfish have long spines protruding from their pectorals that can cause a very painful wound. Sculpin and other small fish are likewise armored. Most bass, perch, and ocean rockfish have fins with sharp spines and very rough skin. If in doubt, handle the fish yourself first.

Many anglers today practice catch and release angling. Some fisheries require the release of certain species, or of wild fish. Or your catch may be too small or too large to keep according to regulations.

If your intention is catch and release fishing, you should use barbless hooks and artificial lures instead of bait. It is extremely rare for a fish to swallow an artificial lure or fly, since the fish will usually spit out plastic lunches. Most are hooked in the lip or jaw. Bait, on the other hand, is real food and is generally swallowed quickly, which embeds the hook deep in the fish's stomach. Barbless hooks will make live release much easier, and are required in most waters that are reserved for catch and release angling.

If you and the angler decide to allow the catch to grow and fight another day, additional handling considerations are in

Brett Brower
age 10

order. The less friction against skin and gills, the better the odds of the fish making a full recovery. If at all possible, keep the fish in the water. If you can reach in and pull the hook out with a pair of pliers or a hook-out, the fish will not have been touched and will probably be fine. If you do have to touch the fish, wet your hands first to minimize friction.

If the fish is hooked deeply in the mouth, you may have to net it and spend a little time working on the hook. Keeping the fish in the net will constrain it somewhat, and make it less likely to injure itself during handling. If possible, keep the net and fish in the water, and don't work on the hook unless the fish is still. I have found that some species of fish are pretty tough and can take considerable handling without ill effect. Trout and other salmonids are very delicate. Even so, with proper handling nine out of ten will survive unhooking.

A fish with torn, bleeding gills will rarely survive. This is one fish to keep if regulations allow. In the unfortunate event that the fish is hooked deeply, both you and the fish are better off if you just cut the line near the hook and release the fish. While the hook may cause death, your efforts to dig down and get it out surely will be fatal. Hooks are actually broken down rapidly by a fish's body tissues. I have caught healthy sturgeon with leaders coming out of their anal vent. When I cleaned the fish, I found that the hook in the fish's stomach was almost completely dissolved.

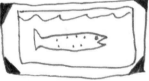

Allison Wong
age 9

12
Invite a Fish Home for Dinner

Cleaning and Preserving the Catch

Oregon Dept. of Fish and Wildlife

While some young anglers might be distressed by the actual act of dispatching the catch, others may well be reluctant to let their hard-won prize go! One satisfactory compromise might be the bucket aquarium.

On outings where the kids and I are going after perch and bluegill just for the fun of the catch, we'll usually take along a bucket. When the first little fish is landed, I'll fill the bucket and plop the catch in. The kids can watch the fish swim around for a few minutes, and then I let them dump it back in the lake. My kids love to watch the little fish swim away. Don't leave it in the bucket for very long, or let the kids grab it or poke it with sticks, and it will be able to continue its adventures after release.

If you are planning on keeping the fish for food, come to the waters prepared. There are several ways to insure the quality of fish for later eating. The first is to keep the fish alive. Once any animal dies, it will start to decompose, and its flesh will lose some of its quality. Fish can be kept alive, if carefully handled. On boats especially equipped for this purpose, the catch is kept in a live well, a tank of oxygenated water.

A less costly investment is a wire mesh basket that can be lowered into the lake or stream with the catch inside. Be sure that the fish have room to move.

The most popular method used to keep fish in the water is a stringer. A stringer can be anything from a length of rope to a small chain with a number of large snaps attached. The line or the snaps are run through the gills to hold each fish in place. The fish are then returned to the waters until time to head for home.

While stringers will work for a while with the more durable species, in most cases the fish will die before it's time to go. A fish's gills are its equivalent of lungs and are the most delicate organ in its body. Run a line through the gills and they won't last long. A stringer tossed back in the water will keep the fish wet and out of the way, but don't count on it keeping them alive. Also, if there are turtles in your waters, an untended stringer of fish can make a dandy meal for them.

If you really want to insure good eating, clean the fish soon after it is caught and put it on ice. Gutting a fish is a very easy process. Not only does immediate cleaning insure a good quality fish for the table, kids find it an interesting process, and it can be quite educational.

To clean a fish, stick the point of a sharp knife into the anal vent, and cut the fish all the way to the gills. Then put your finger all the way to the fish's backbone and pull out all the guts. (Kids love this part.) With a little practice, you will be able to show them the heart, liver, and stomach. For many youngsters, fish provide their first opportunity to learn a little anatomy. Finally, it is a good idea to scrape the purple material off the inside of the backbone (the kidneys). After the entrails are removed and the cavity is

HOW TO CLEAN A TROUT

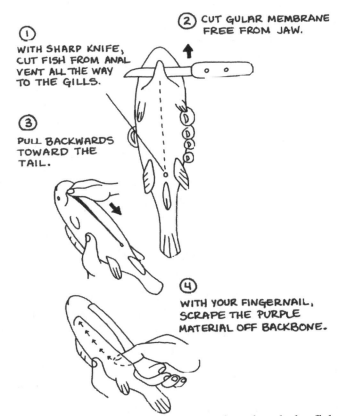

① WITH SHARP KNIFE, CUT FISH FROM ANAL VENT ALL THE WAY TO THE GILLS.

② CUT GULAR MEMBRANE FREE FROM JAW.

③ PULL BACKWARDS TOWARD THE TAIL.

④ WITH YOUR FINGERNAIL, SCRAPE THE PURPLE MATERIAL OFF BACKBONE.

thoroughly washed in whatever water is at hand, the fish should be packed in ice and stored for the trip home. A little crushed ice, both in the cavity and over the fish, will prevent deterioration and insure good eating.

Traditionally, anglers kept the catch in a wicker creel covered with a little streamside vegetation. While this kept the fish moist for a time, it did not serve well in the long run. Many fish that taste muddy or soft were simply improperly preserved. Clean the fish immediately, and put it on ice.

Blue ice containers kept in many ice chests also work well. Put the fish in the bottom of the chest next to the blue ice, and cover the whole works with an insulator such as newspaper or paper towels.

Your young doctors might also learn a little something from exploring the contents of the fish's stomach. Fly anglers routinely examine fish stomachs to determine the best fly to offer. Youngsters can learn a lot about a fish's eating habits through the process. Fortunately, fresh fish odor is inoffensive, so the dissection is not particularly distasteful unless one is really squeamish. Slit open the stomach and squeeze the contents into a shallow, white container. A dish or even a pickle jar cap will serve. Add a bit of water and swirl the contents. You and the kids should be able to identify what the fish recently had for a snack.

Disposal of innards is a bit of a problem in some waters. If you are fishing a busy streamside, you might consider bagging the entrails and disposing of them in the nearest garbage can. The sight of fish guts on the bank or streambed is less than inspiring to fellow anglers (though in reality, they are part of the more-or-less natural system and will quickly be recycled by local birds, fish, and raccoons). If the stream is heavily fished, they should be removed. Some areas actually have laws prohibiting fish cleaning on site, so be aware of the local requirements, and use common sense.

When fishing in lakes, rivers, or on the ocean, fish are routinely cleaned on board, and the entrails dropped into the waters. Gulls and terns make quick work of most material thrown overboard, and fish and crabs will fight over the rest.

13
I Caught It and We Ate It

Cooking Tips

Dan Casali

Fish is an excellent food. Not only does it provide protein that the body can readily use, but it is also low in cholesterol and fat. Fish oils have been shown to actually reduce blood cholesterol levels. Dieticians and medical professionals praise the value of fish for a healthy diet. You'll be doing your children a lifelong favor if you teach them to enjoy eating fish.

Most kids get pretty excited about the prospect of eating something they have caught, gathered, or grown themselves. The hunter-gatherer instinct is strong, and children are generally enthusiastic about helping to provide for the family. Encourage this attitude by making a fuss over their catch and by cooking just about anything they really want to eat. It is almost impossible to find a fish that is not edible, and even tasty. Some fish are easier to clean than others, but just about all will taste fine if cleaned, preserved, and cooked properly.

Fresh caught fish make the tastiest meals. Fish that go into the freezer may develop long frosty beards before they come out, and the flavor and texture of the meat will suffer. The kids will usually want their catch cooked up as soon as possible in any event.

Cooking fish demands a little more attention and is a bit more time consuming than just whipping up a little Hamburger Helper™. My first rule in preparing fish for kids is: get rid of the bones. No matter how great the stuff tastes, a small bone in the throat will ruin the experience. A little later in the game, kids will enjoy the challenge of picking through the fish to remove all the bones, but wait till they are hooked on the taste and really enjoy eating fish.

The best way to insure that no bones are present is to fillet the fish. This process involves cutting the fish so that the meat from its sides are stripped off the bone. There are a number of ways to cut a fillet, depending on the shape and size of the fish. In most cases, the knife is pressed flat against the narrow strip of flesh just above the fish's tail. A cut is made into the flesh up against, but not penetrating, the backbone. You then cut on the backbone down the fish to the gills. Then remove the knife, and cut diagonally along the gill flap to free the piece of flesh. Finally, cut the flesh free from the skin.

Properly done, the fillet will be free of all bones and will contain most of the meat available. Carefully examine the fillet for bones, using both your eyes and your fingers, before cooking. While the amount of meat recovered depends on the species, a rule of thumb is that one third of a fish's weight can be recovered in edible fillet. Smaller fish may have a lower percentage, but even sloppy surgery should result in at least twenty-five percent recovery.

No doubt about it, filleting fish is a real art. In our neck of the woods, many folks are employed in the fish process-

PREPARING A FILLET

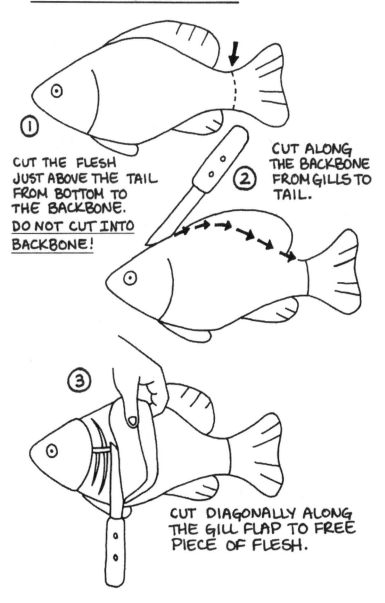

① CUT THE FLESH JUST ABOVE THE TAIL FROM BOTTOM TO THE BACKBONE. <u>DO NOT CUT INTO BACKBONE!</u>

② CUT ALONG THE BACKBONE FROM GILLS TO TAIL.

③ CUT DIAGONALLY ALONG THE GILL FLAP TO FREE PIECE OF FLESH.

ing business. A good filleter can do wonders with a sharp thin knife and is much in demand. I'm sure that your kids will enjoy watching you work on the fish, and as they get a little older, they can try their own hand at it. My kids love watching mom work on the fish, or watching me slicing away, telling me how mom does it better (unfortunately true!).

Many fish commonly taken by kids are a little too small to fillet easily. Panfish and trout are best prepared by frying them in a hot buttered skillet. After a minute or so on each side, the meat can be flaked off the bones with a fork.

Flaking easily is the test for readiness. If the meat still sticks to the bones, it needs to cook a little longer. Over cooking is also a problem with many fish. Cook the fish too long, and it's hard to tell fish from bones!

Once the meat flakes off easily and has a nice firm texture, it can be served with tartar sauce or catsup, or in melted butter with lemon and almond slices.

Be sure to have plenty of other favorite foods as well as fish on the menu. Let the kids develop a taste for fish gradually. Many new foods take a little time to get used to, and fish is no exception. Don't force kids to eat more than they want. Even if one bite seems to be as much as they care to eat, make a big deal over how great their fish was. They will remember the whole event in a positive light and look forward to their next fish dinner.

There are many excellent ways to prepare fish. Some of our favorites are fillets dipped in beer batter and deep fried, or cut into chunks and simmered in a white chowder with bacon and sour cream, or cut into steaks and barbecued over hot coals. In addition, we have our own smoker and have yet to find a variety of fish that doesn't taste great with a little apple wood smoke. Any fish that you keep should be eaten, so give a little thought to the care and preparation of your catch. Children can be taught to enjoy the flavor of fish, and you can help by developing a little expertise in the kitchen.

Meghan McDonald
age 9

EASY KITCHEN OR CAMPFIRE RECIPES

FRIED FILLETS

1. DIP FILLETS IN MILK, BUTTERMILK, OR EGG
2. THEN ROLL IN FLOUR, BISQUIT MIX, CORN MEAL, OR BREAD CRUMBS SEASONED WITH SALT & PEPPER
3. HEAT OIL IN SKILLET AND FRY TILL BROWN, TURNING ONCE
4. SERVE WITH TARTAR SAUCE

TARTAR SAUCE

MIX 1 CUP MAYONNAISE OR SALAD DRESSING, WITH 1/4 CUP PICKLE RELISH (OR 1 TEASPOON DILL WEED), 2 TEASPOONS LEMON JUICE, 2 TABLESPOONS MINCED ONION (OR 1/2 TEASPOON ONION POWDER), AND 1 TEASPOON DRIED PARSLEY FLAKES

GRILLED TROUT IN BACON

1. WRAP EACH WHOLE CLEANED TROUT IN A STRIP OF THIN SLICED BACON
2. PLACE TROUT ON NARROW-MESH GRILL OVER LOW FIRE OR HOT COALS
3. TURN ONCE USING TWO PANCAKE TURNERS
4. FISH IS DONE WHEN BACON IS CRISP
5. REMOVE BONES
6. SERVE WITH A SQUIRT OF FRESH LEMON, SALT & PEPPER

MORE RECIPES FOR KITCHEN OR CAMPFIRE

FISH CHOWDER

8 STRIPS BACON
1 LARGE ONION, DICED
2 QUARTS MILK
2 TABLESPOONS FLOUR
6 LARGE POTATOS
2 CUPS FRESH MUSHROOMS, SLICED
4 CUPS SOUR CREAM
¼ CUP SHERRY (OPTIONAL)
1-1½ POUNDS DICED FISH

BROWN BACON, ADD ONION, AND SIMMER. STIR IN FLOUR, MILK, AND POTATOS. COOK ON MEDIUM HEAT UNTIL POTATOS ARE SOFT. ADD MUSHROOMS, SOUR CREAM, SHERRY, AND FISH. COOK UNTIL FISH IS DONE. DO NOT BOIL.

FILLETS DEEP FRIED IN BEER BATTER

2 EGGS
1-12 OZ. CAN OF BEER
1 CUP FLOUR
1 TEASPOON BAKING POWDER
1 TEASPOON SALT
PEPPER TO TASTE

SEPARATE EGGS. BEAT YOLK USING WHISK. ADD BEER, FLOUR, BAKING POWDER, SALT AND PEPPER. STIR TILL BATTER IS SMOOTH. FOLD IN STIFFLY BEATEN EGG WHITES. LET STAND AT ROOM TEMPERATURE 30 MINUTES BEFORE USING. DIP FISH (AND SLICED FRESH VEGETABLES!) IN BATTER AND FRY IN 2 INCHES OIL AT 250° TILL CRISP AND BROWN.

SAUTEED TROUT

1. MELT BUTTER IN SKILLET
2. SAUTE SLICED ONIONS (GREEN PEPPERS AND FRESH GARLIC ARE GOOD, TOO) TILL SOFT
3. MOVE VEGETABLES TO ONE SIDE AND ADD WHOLE CLEANED TROUT, SPREADING VEGETABLES OVER FISH
4. FISH IS DONE WHEN MEAT FLAKES EASILY
5. REMOVE BONES
6. SERVE WITH A SQUIRT OF FRESH LEMON, SALT & PEPPER

Jenni Ashcroft
age 10

14
Keeping Kids
Hooked on Fishing

Attention Getters

Bill Wagner

Kids have a lot of energy and a limited attention span. Unless you know a spot with a million hungry fish, there will be times when the action is slow. Even if you find great fishing, most kids will eventually grow tired of the activity and look for something else to do! Every fishing trip with small fry really should be approached as a varied outing, with plenty of built-in flexibility, and a few special games and activities planned to augment the angling.

When we go to lakes, rivers, or bays, we usually take along a little bacon and try for a few crawdads. These red crustaceans inhabit most warm water lakes and streams and provide an exciting diversion. You can either use a little string with the bait tied on one end, or some sort of commercial or homemade crawdad trap. Lower the bait to the bottom, let it sit for a few minutes, and pull it back in. We've caught up to a hundred of these "mini-lobsters" on a good day, and sometimes they are they only thing we catch that's suitable for dinner!

My youngsters love to look for bugs, and most fishy locations offer excellent "bugging" opportunities. Take along an empty jar for the collecting efforts. Insects can either be collected as bait, or just for the joy of it. You can join in the fun by identifying the critters collected, or by offering suggestions as to where others may be found.

When I was a kid, my Grandpa always used to take an axe with us when we went trout fishing. If the action slowed, we'd find a rotted log and hack away, ostensibly looking for grubs to use as bait. I really can't remember if we caught much on the little white blobs, but we sure had a good time busting up logs!

Many lake shores and stream banks also offer great opportunities for butterfly netting. We had a big collection of butterflies on grandma's pantry wall. Many of the prize specimens were discovered far away from home at mountain lakes and streams. Our nets were the homemade variety—bent clothes hangers draped with mosquito netting, and an old broom handle to give us height. Chasing through meadows was a highlight of many of our outdoor adventures.

Amphibians and reptiles always draw a lot of interest from the junior set. That empty fish bucket makes a wonder-

Alex Yoder
age 8

ful temporary aquarium or terrarium for collection and observation of creepy, crawly creatures. During our fishing adventures, my kids have captured several kinds of salamanders and frogs, assorted snakes, lizards, and eels.

I keep a collection of good field guides in the glove box of my truck. With this tiny library I can help the boys identify the plants, flowers, amphibians, reptiles, birds, and insects of our region. The Audubon Society produces my favorite collection, but a number of good guides are available for virtually every section of the country.

When the fishing slows, it's also a good time to slip in a little "sneaky learning." How many plants and flowers can they collect and identify? How many birds fly by your fishing hole and what varieties? Are those swallows nesting now, or are they traveling somewhere else? Most books include a few choice paragraphs describing the life cycle of each species or offer other interesting tidbits to share with the kids.

Wherever you fish, you will find abundant plant and animal life, and lots of natural beauty to enjoy and explain. I make it a point to take a seminar a year at our local community college.

Elena Puha
age 11

Fishing with Small Fry

In the past few years I have developed some expertise on local tidepools, plant life, forest composition, wild flowers, berries, and even edible mushrooms.

You'll be amazed at how much information your kids will pick up from your "classrooms in the wild." My six year old is an accomplished mushroom fancier. He is much better than I at digging under the brush for select species and, in fact, prefers our "shrooming outings" to either hunting or fishing! (Don't try to learn your mushrooms from a book; there are mushrooms that can kill you. Go out with an expert.)

As children get older, they can enjoy exploring a wealth of reading material on their own. Magazines and books offer fishing and outdoor tips to novice and expert alike. While my kids are too young to do much reading at this point, they love looking through outdoor magazines, enjoying the photos of critters, vehicles, and boats. There are also several outdoor magazines written especially for children. Check the children's room at your local library for sample copies.

Don't overlook those obvious activities that are available near the water. Remember to plan for a varied outing, not just a fishing trip. If the weather is hot and the water is safe, go out and splash with the kids. So you scare the fish—you should have caught them in the morning anyway! And besides, they'll recover in time for the evening rise. Of course, you must keep a close eye on the youngsters when they're in the water. Make sure they don't get in over their heads or beyond your capacity to rescue them.

Finally, encourage your kids in whatever activity they may find interesting. If they want to dig in the mud on the riverbank, loan them a spoon and a bucket. If they want to build a fort out of driftwood, show a little interest. Don't insist that all of their attention be devoted to fishing.

Remember, the whole purpose of the outing is to encourage them to enjoy the outdoors and to develop a positive attitude toward the sport. If you let them do so at their own pace, and in their own way, they'll treasure the time they spent with you and love you for it.

And before you know it, that day will arrive when you toss your gear into the trunk of their car and "go fishing with the kids."

Tanasha Mason
age 8

About The Author

Claudia Ellsberg

Bob Ellsberg is irrepressible, a cascade of enthusiasm for his obsessions—fishing and hunting, storytelling, and teaching.

Born in Vallejo, California and educated near the rich waters of the Sacramento River, Bob was rarely far from a fishing rod. After a decade of public service as a police officer and teacher in the San Francisco Bay area, he tired of the traffic and chaos, and headed for the more peaceful (and fishful) geography of Astoria in northwestern Oregon, where he lives with his wife, Claudia, and their two children.

In Oregon, Bob found he could blend his commitments to public service and the outdoors. He has conducted classes in fishing and in woodlands ecology for the Boy Scouts and for the Oregon Department of Fish and Wildlife. He serves on the Oregon State Parks Advisory Committee, and was Vice President of the Columbia River Estuary Task Force.

From his office at Clatsop Community College, where he is Director of Cooperative Education, Bob keeps an eye on the mighty Columbia River—inspiration for frequent fishing adventures and for his weekly outdoors column for the *Daily Astorian*, "On the Outside."

Other books by Bob Ellsberg:
> *Steelheading for the Simple-minded*
> *Salmon Fishing for the Simple-minded*